Modern Funk Bass

The Method

– By Ivan Lombardi –

Woodshed Academy

First paperback edition January 2024

ISBN 979-8-9883266-0-1

www.woodshedacademy.com

CONTENTS

LESSON 13

LESSON 14

LESSON 15

ETUDES

APPENDICIES

A WORD FROM THE AUTHOR

When I was a young aspiring bass player, Funk was one of the styles I loved playing the most. In fact, it was one of the reasons I chose to play the bass in the first place. I had a strong desire to learn everything I could about Funk and eagerly purchased almost every available book on the market.

However, I often found myself wanting more from these books. They mostly consisted of song transcriptions, which were undoubtedly fun to play, but didn't offer much in terms of learning value for me. As an ambitious learner, I wanted to delve deeper into creating my own bass lines. To do that, I knew I needed to understand concepts like harmony, scales, rhythms, playing techniques, and more.

Over time, I developed into a creative bass player who could write my own bass lines and music. Nevertheless, I couldn't help but think about how much time I could have saved with the right quality instruction. Inspired by this, I decided to embark on a project and write a method for modern Funk bass, the kind of resource I wish I had more than 35 years ago!

This method consists of fifteen detailed lessons that gradually teach the core musical concepts necessary to master the art of modern Funk bass. Each lesson is supplemented with numerous examples to reinforce the concepts being taught. Additionally, I have included ten Funk bass Etudes (Studies) for practice, which will showcase the potential of the techniques and concepts presented in the course.

To ensure the best learning experience, I have utilized the latest available technologies. The course combines well-structured written lessons with video examples and high-quality audio backing tracks recorded by professional studio musicians. All of this is presented in a state-of-the-art learning platform.

My hope is that you will thoroughly enjoy this course, just as I have enjoyed creating it. And if, by the end of it, you feel that your Funk bass musical skills have improved, you are having more fun playing, and you are able to create your own bass lines, then I will have achieved the objective of this book.

Happy learning, and enjoy the journey!

HOW TO USE THIS BOOK

This book has been specifically designed to be used as a semester-long course, suitable for music academies or colleges. It consists of 15 progressive lessons that introduce and advance through the necessary harmonic and rhythmic concepts for mastering modern Funk bass.

Each lesson incorporates multiple musical examples that are carefully crafted to illustrate the application of the discussed techniques. The tablature provided serves as a reference on the fretboard, guiding you on how to play the bass lines. It is crucial to watch and imitate the fingerings and hand positions demonstrated in the accompanying video examples, as they will assist you in developing the technique required to tackle more complex examples in the Etudes section.

In addition to the lessons, there is a series of rhythmic exercises included in Appendix A. These exercises can be utilized to reinforce your understanding and mastery of the rhythmic patterns introduced in each lesson. It is recommended to work through each exercise or employ them as self-assessment tools.

Once you have completed the lessons, it is highly encouraged to regularly play and practice the Etudes. These pieces are both fun to play and serve as excellent examples of how to apply what you have learned throughout the course. By engaging with the Etudes, you will solidify your understanding of the concepts and techniques covered.

Remember, consistent practice and application of the material is key to your growth as a Funk bass player.

ETUDES

In this section, you will find ten Funk Etudes (a musical term for studies) in different keys. They are written to show the use of the harmonic and rhythmic concepts from the lessons in extended grooves of 32 measures.

The studies are structured into four main sections of eight measures each:

- **Section A** lays down the main groove and its fundamental rhythmic and harmonic structure.

- **Section B** demonstrate how to add variety and create a intricate bass line by adding rhythmic variations.

- **Section C** adds further variety and often introduces the use of double stops.

- **Section D** focuses on fills, featuring one measure of a groove and one measure of fill. These fills incorporate a mix of scales and chromatic patterns.

Each section progressively becomes more technically demanding. It is essential to take your time and practice each section slowly and accurately, paying attention to proper fingering and hand position.

There are a few recommended approaches for practicing the Etudes. One method is to focus on a single study at a time, working on it until you have mastered it before moving on to the next one. Another approach is to focus on all the A sections of each Etude first and gradually add the remaining sections, such as the B section, then the C section, and so on. The choice of approach is yours and depends on your preference and learning style.

On the companion website, you will find video examples of the Etudes performed at the final tempo, allowing you to observe the proper execution of the pieces. Additionally, there are backing tracks available for practice, which can be adjusted to a slower tempo if necessary.

VIDEO EXAMPLES AND BACKING TRACKS

Whenever you come across this ▶ icon in the book, it indicates that there is a corresponding video example available for viewing on the website www.woodshedacademy.com. To access these videos, simply enroll in the free course titled "Modern Funk Bass - Free Video Examples".

By doing so, you will have the opportunity to fully utilize the video player, access the accompanying backing tracks, and track your progress thru the lessons.

Additional online lessons

As an added resource, we offer an online version of this course titled " Modern Funk Bass - Guided Sessions." In this online course, the author personally delivers the lessons, providing a more comprehensive and in-depth explanation of the concepts and techniques covered in the book. The author takes the opportunity to delve into greater detail and explore the nuances of each topic.

Moreover, the online course includes a harmonic breakdown and analysis of all the studies presented. This analysis offers valuable insights into the underlying musical structure and helps you understand the harmonic choices made in each piece.

By enrolling in the "Modern Funk Bass - Guided Sessions," you can benefit from the author's expertise and gain a deeper understanding of the material. The online format allows for a more immersive learning experience, enhancing your ability to grasp and apply the concepts and techniques taught in the course.

About the Author

Ivan Lombardi began his professional career as a bass player in the vibrant music scene of Los Angeles. He graduated from the Musician Institute with a distinguished 'Vocational with Honors' recognition.

Seeking new opportunities, he later relocated to Europe and established himself as a versatile freelance musician, participating in numerous tours, TV shows, studio sessions, and collaborations with acclaimed artists such as Lilian Boutte, Eric Marienthal, Gene Calderazzo, Franco Ambrosetti, Mitchell Forman, Ralph Humphrey, Eileina Dennis, Rick Margitza, Jon Davies, Jeff Richman, Martha Duarte, Judith Emeline and many others.

Driven by a passion for continuous growth, he pursued further education and obtained a degree in Music Pedagogy from the classical conservatory of Lugano in Switzerland and a Master's Degree in Double Bass Performance from the conservatory of Pavia, Italy.

Under the mentorship of the late Dick Grove, founder of the Grove School of Music in Los Angeles, Ivan studied jazz composition and arrangement.

Having served as the Musical Director for a Swiss Italian Big Band for eight years, Ivan later relocated to Asia, where he continued to pursue his artistic endeavors in bass improvisation, education, composition, arranging, and further honing his piano skills.

For those seeking to connect with Ivan, he can be reached through various social media channels or contacted via email at info@woodshedacademy.com.

Aknowledgments

A heartfelt word of gratitude to Pancho Ragonese (keyboards) and Francesca Prattico (drums), two remarkable and talented musicians who professionally recorded the backing tracks. Special thanks to Oliver Nash for his valuable expertise and beautiful graphic design, Dr. Andrea Pobanz for her essential didactical suggestions and to Raymond Tognola for the contagious motivation and brainstorming sessions at the inception of this project.

LESSON

Objectives

- Understand the rhythmic foundations of funk bass
- Learn the first two 16th notes rhythmic patterns
- Recognize and apply the new 16th notes patterns

Understand the Rhythmic Foundation of Funk Bass

To play Funk grooves on the bass or any instrument, the most crucial skill a musician must possess is the ability to play and feel sixteenth-note rhythmic patterns with precision and timing. In Funk bass, rhythm is paramount; it's all about capturing the right rhythmic feel and executing it tightly (in the pocket). In the early lessons, our primary focus will be on mastering fundamental rhythmic patterns.

The process of learning these rhythms follows a specific approach: first, we isolate the individual rhythmic patterns and practice them with a single note until they become internalized. Then, we progress to applying these patterns to actual grooves.

But fear not! There is much more to explore beyond rhythmic patterns. As you advance through the lessons, you will delve into scale sources, technique, chromaticism, chords, and arpeggios. These elements will expand your creativity and make you proficient in creating Funk bass lines and grooves.

16th Note Rhythmic Patterns

Now, let's dive into the realm of 16th note rhythmic patterns. We'll begin with the first pattern!

Note: When you see the display icon ▶ in the examples, go to www.woodshedacademy.com, make sure to select the free 'Modern Funk Bass - Free Video Examples' course and watch the corresponding examples. Take your time to get acquainted with the platform's structure, features, and the video player.

▶ **Example 1.1: Rhythmic Pattern 1**

Now it is your turn. Practice this rhythm with the drum track track until you feel comfortable playing it.

Tip: When you practice with the backing tracks on the website, take full advantage of the capability of the embedded player, where you can slow down or speed up the track to match your current level!

Time to apply what we just learned in a simple groove.

Example 1.2: Groove with Rhythmic Pattern 1

When practicing this groove, pay attention to two things:

1. When playing in the lower register with the left hand, it is best to utilize the fingering 1-2-4. This allows you to play in a more relaxed way, rather than using 1-2-3 fingering which requires a large stretch and puts more stress on the hand. Using 1-2-4 makes it easier to play notes in adjacent frets and allows the hand to relax.

2. The start of the 16th note pattern. In this case, the 2nd and 4th beat of the measures is different from the initial example but has the same rhythm.

Tip: When you practice a new groove in the lessons, If you are having difficulties practicing them, try playing a single note (in this case C) with the same rhythm as the groove you're working on. This will help solidify the rhythm before adding in the notes.

Let's move on to the second pattern.

Example 1.3: Rhythmic Pattern 2

This pattern is made up of the first two 16th notes of Rhythmic Pattern 1, and it always starts on the downbeat in a measure, in this case, on beats 1 and 3.

Let's apply it to the previous groove to make it more interesting!

Example 1.4: Groove with Rhythmic Pattern 2

Notice the rhythmic similarity of the patterns from the previous groove but how they are positioned differently in the measures.

To complete this lesson, let's practice a few more grooves!

▶ Example 1.5: Groove with Rhythmic Pattern 2

Make sure to play this grove with the same fingering used in the video.

▶ Example 1.6: Groove with Rhythmic Pattern 2

Tip: The last two grooves are a little more difficult as they introduce an octave skip. If this causes you trouble, play only the root and omit the octave skip until you are ready to add it in.

SUMMARY

- **Understand the significance of recognizing and playing different sixteenth-note rhythmic patterns in order to create Funk bass lines.**

- **Focus on mastering the initial two rhythmic patterns and incorporate them into grooves, utilizing accompanying backing tracks for practice.**

- **Get acquainted with using the online platform as a valuable resource to enhance your learning experience.**

LESSON

- **Learn to play rhythmic patterns starting on the upbeat**
- **Practice grooves with the rhythmic patterns learned thus far**
- **Learn about Creative Practice**

2

UPBEAT RHYTHMIC PATTERNS

In this second lesson, the focus is on an essential skill: playing rhythmic patterns starting on the upbeat.

In music, the first beat of a measure is the downbeat. Downbeats are strong and often mark the first part (half) of the beat, whereas the upbeat marks the second part (half) of it. When we tap our foot along with the music, we naturally tap loudest on the downbeat. The upbeat - which we will focus on in this lesson - leads to the downbeat and alerts us to the fact that a downbeat is coming. Upbeats drive movement in music and play an important role that can bring more life to our performance.

A good way to practice and develop the feel of downbeats and upbeats is to tap your foot along with the music. When counting in 4/4 time, we would say '1 and 2 and 3 and 4.' The downbeats would be all the numbers (foot down), while the upbeats would be every occurrence of 'and' (toe up).

Let's practice tapping the beats in the following example.

▶ Example 2.1: Downbeats and Upbeats

This technique is not too difficult, however, take the time to practice it until it becomes fluid (you can find additional reading exercises in Appendix A). It will serve you well when the grooves become more rhythmically complex!

Tip: Note that upbeats can either be an eighth or sixteenth note. Downbeats and upbeats will not always follow a specific pattern.

Let's now learn the new rhythmic pattern with this technique.

▶ Example 2.2: Rhythmic Pattern 3

Notice how the two sixteenth notes are both played on the upbeat, when your foot should be elevated.

Let's play grooves with the patterns you have learned.

▶ Example 2.3: Groove with Rhythmic Pattern 3

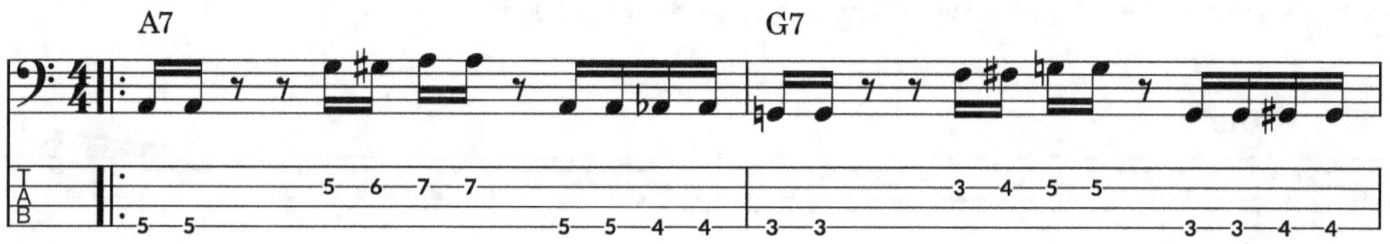

Rhythmic patterns 2 and 3 are common but are worth practicing. In the following new patterns, an eight-note has been added.

▶ Example 2.4: Rhythmic Pattern 4

▶ Example 2.5: Rhythmic Pattern 5

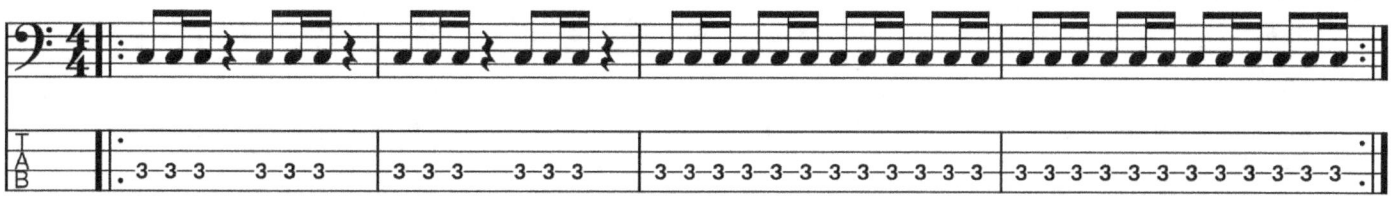

Our rhythmic vocabulary with sixteenth-note patterns is expanding, and it will allow you to create more interesting bass lines.

Tip: After you have practiced the patterns in this lesson, check out Appendix A.
Several rhythmic studies have been added for your practice to reinforce the learning.
Is also a way to test yourself and understand which patterns should be given more attention until they are fully learned!

▶ **Example 2.6: Groove with Rhythmic Patterns 4 & 5**

In this groove, the five patterns you have learned are utilized. Do you recognize them?

The first measure uses patterns 1 & 2, the second measure adds pattern 3, and the last two measures include patterns 4 and 5.

Let's practice one more groove!

▶ **Example 2.7: Groove with Rhythmic Patterns 4 & 5**

In this example, you can use either the A open string or the A on the E string; both are easily playable.

Tip: When you have mastered the groove, try to play the octaves of some or all of the repeated notes. This will add interest to the line and build up your technique!

CREATIVE PRACTICE

Creative practice is an important concept that will allow you to learn how to create original bass lines easily when practiced regularly.
Try improvising spontaneously what you have learned, in this case, you would improvise with the five rhythmic patterns you have learned so far.

Indeed you can add quarter notes and octaves, but mostly try to use the sixteenth-note patterns you have learned so far. The goal is to reinforce them until they become natural, and you can play them without thinking.

Since you haven't yet learned about harmony, use a single note to improvise on the patterns when you practice. The goal is to create rhythms spontaneously before learning and incorporating chord tones, diatonic and chromatic notes.

Example 2.8: Creative Practice with All the Rhythmic Patterns

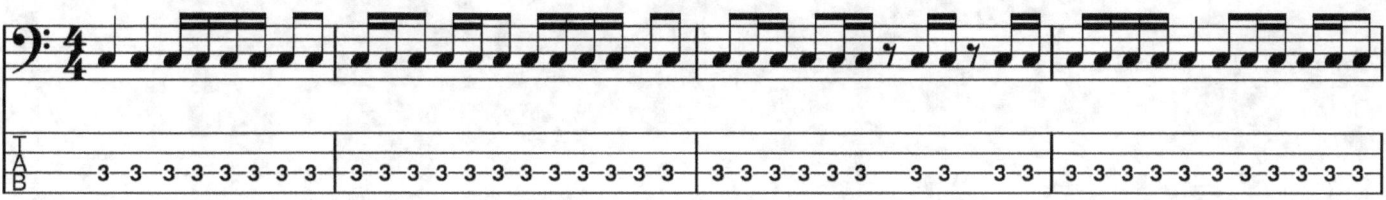

The rhythm above is improvised, and while using the backing track, you can progressively improvise the rhythms you have already learned.

Tip: If improvising using all the patterns is too demanding, simply practice with only patterns 1 and 2. Once you are comfortable with those, you can add in Patterns 3 through 5 one at a time until you are comfortable incorporating some or all of them at the same time.

SUMMARY

- **Practice and learn the concept of the upbeat using the foot-tapping technique. This technique will be a reference point for more complex rhythm patterns.**

- **Learn rhythmic patterns 3, 4, and 5 and apply them to grooves.**

- **Use Creative Practice on rhythmic patterns as a tool to develop musical creativity.**

LESSON

Objectives

- **Learn the Dominant 7th chord**
- **Learn the first chromatic passing note**
- **Creative practice**

3

THE DOMINANT 7TH CHORD

Of all the chords used in Funk tunes, the 7th chord (also called the dominant chord) is the most used due to its sounds. The study and practice of its arpeggio is a good starting point to understand the relationship between harmony and the bass line, and later on, it will be the tool to create bass lines spontaneously.

It is essential to understand why we don't learn to play or create funk grooves with a scale as the primary reference and instead we begin with an arpeggio. This is because not all the seven notes of a scale have the same importance harmonically as the four notes of a chord, that are the root (1), 3rd, 5th, and 7th.

To clarify, harmonies played by a guitarist or a keyboardist always contain the essential notes of the chords (especially the 3rd and 7th). As bass players, our musical role is to highlight the harmonies in a rhythmic and funky way. Therefore, it is necessary to use at least a few (if not all) chord tones as the primary source to create bass lines.

To learn which notes to use and which additional non-chord notes to add, keep reading and discover them in the following lessons!

Let's see in practice how a 7th chord arpeggio sounds like!

▶ Example 3.1: The G7 Arpeggio

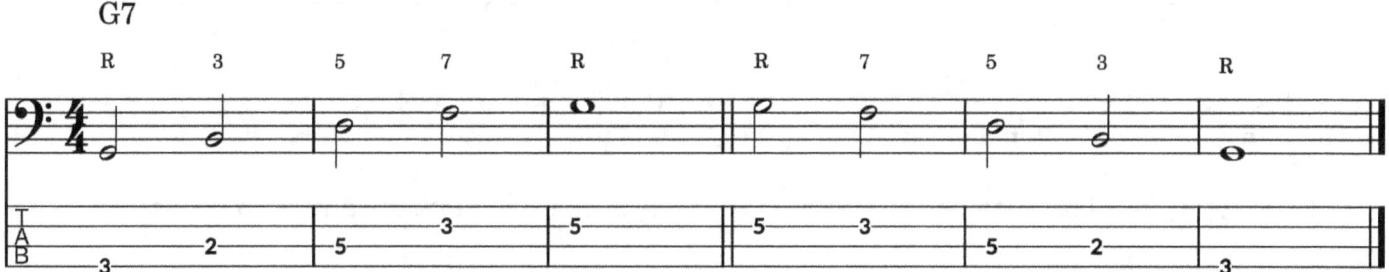

The 7th chord is built with the following intervals: root - major 3rd - perfect 5th - minor 7th

Formula: The fingering to play this arpeggio is **2-1-4-2-4.** This is valid to use for all dominant 7th arpeggios, try it with a different root using the same formula.

We can now create and play bass lines with the notes of the 7th arpeggio as the example below.

▶ Example 3.2: Groove with G7 Dominant 7th Chord Tones

CHROMATIC PATTERNS

Chromatic notes are notes that are not part of the chord or the scale, and provide an exciting sound to the bass lines.

There are five chromatic notes that can be used. These notes have the function of connecting by half-step the various chord tones.

At this point, we will focus mainly the tones of the 7th chord, as in example 3.1. Once you have mastered all five chromatic possibilities on this chord, we will apply our knowledge to other types of chords.

The first chromatic passing note connects the 7th of the chord and the root, which we call chromatic pattern 1.

▶ Example 3.3: Chromatic Pattern 1

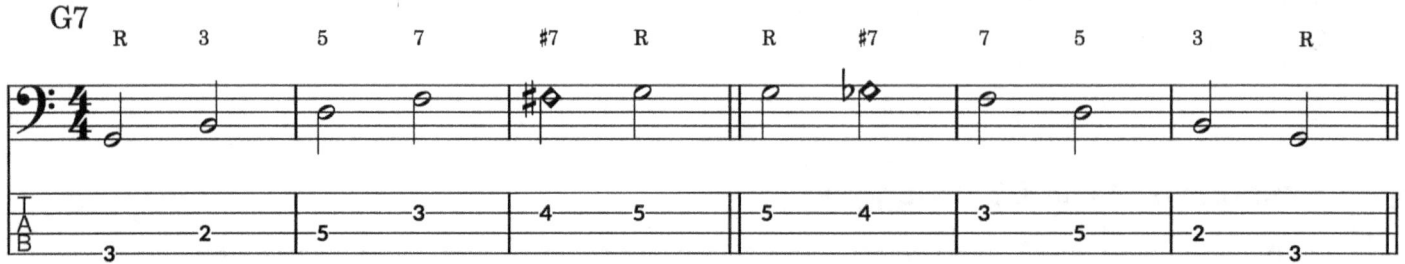

The chromatic note in Example 3.3 is the one with the diamond shape-note head, and like any chromatic note, it can have two names, in this case, F♯ and G♭, but it is still the same sound.

Let's apply this chromatic pattern to the previous groove and notice the effect on the sound.

▶ Example 3.4: Groove with Chromatic Pattern 1

In this line, chromatic pattern 1 is used three times. As you can see, the F♯ connects the 7th of the G7 chord (F) and the root (G).

On the last beat of measure 3, we displaced the chromatic note by an octave, as in example 3.2, this can be done with any repeated note, chromatic or not!

Let's look at another arpeggio, this time in E7, we will learn it in two different positions.

▶ Example 3.5: The E7 Arpeggio

Like the G7 arpeggio, the E7 arpeggio uses the basic fingering formula we learned before: **2-1-4-2-4**.

However, the E7 arpeggio has the opportunity to also be fully extended to the lower octave. This will give us many more chord tones to choose from to play groves in E.

▶ Example 3.6: The E7 Arpeggio, Lower Octave

We cannot apply our formula here as the arpeggio starts with an open string.

One good option for fingering would be to play the open string and then use the same fingering for the remaining notes **0-1-4-2-4** (as in the video example).

Let's apply all this new knowledge to make grooves in practice.

▶ Example 3.7: Groove on E7

This groove uses all the elements you have learned so far, the five rhythmic patterns and the new chromatic one. Here, the chromatic note that connects the 7th (D) to the root (E) is the D♯.

Pay attention to the fingering used in the example, as it is the same one used in Lesson 1. The closed hand position with the **1-2-4** fingering played throughout is a comfortable hand position.

Tip: In a live situation where you are playing an entire tune that might last more than 5 minutes, you should aim to have comfortable fingering and hand position to avoid unnecessary effort and strain on the hand and fingers, like is done in the these examples.

▶ Example 3.8: Groove on E7

When practicing this line, take time to recognize the rhythmic pattern, the notes of the 7th chord, and where chromatic pattern 1 is being used between the Root and the 7th of the chord.

SUMMARY

- **Learn how to create bass lines on the most used chord in Funk, the 7th chord, also called the Dominant.**

- **Understand that chord tones are the fundamental building blocks of any bass line. They will be our primary choice when composing new ones.**

- **We introduced the first chromatic pattern between the Root (or tonic) of the chord and the 7th chromatic pattern 1, to create more interesting lines.**

LESSON

- **Learn to play the fourth 16th in the beat**
- **Four new rhythmic patterns**
- **The importance of groove analysis**

4

THE FOURTH 16TH IN THE BEAT

In this lesson, rhythms will start to get quite interesting!

In Lessons 1 and 2, we learned rhythmic patterns that begin on either the downbeat or upbeat of a measure. By now, you should start to have reasonable control of those rhythmic attacks or pulses. Below is a summary.

Example 4.1: Rhythmic Pulses

Notes marked with D are the downbeats, and those with U are the upbeats. The remaining notes are the second and fourth 16th of the beat.

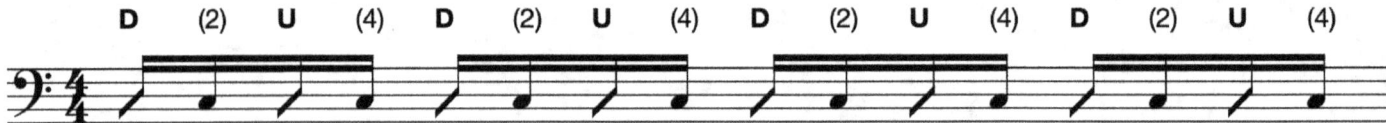

In this lesson, we will focus on the fourth 16th, and as you will see and hear, it will turn up the funk feel of your grooves!

Example 4.2: The Fourth 16ᵗʰ Note In a Beat

Before practicing grooves or the rhythmic patterns that include this figure, it is best to do some preliminary exercises.

In Lesson 2, we introduced the concept of the upbeat and the foot-tapping technique. In this lesson, we will use the same technique to learn this new pattern but with a more specific procedure to help you master this new rhythm.

PRACTICE PROCEDURE

1. We will play the full measure with pattern 1 (playing all 16th notes) and accent the last sixteenth.

Example 4.3: Accented Fourth 16ᵗʰ Note in Pattern 1

2. In this pattern we slowly decrease the volume of the first three notes until only the last 16th note can be heard. This will be our new rhythmic pattern.

Note: We will not use the tablature for rhythmic patterns anymore, as we should be familiar with where to find C.

▶ Example 4.4: Rhythmic Pattern 6

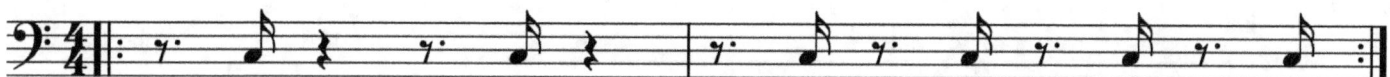

Once you are comfortable practicing this pattern, you can apply it to the next groove.

▶ Example 4.5: Groove with Rhythmic Pattern 6

Remember to play slowly and precisely. For now we want to focus on precision in the execution with the foot-tapping technique and not speed.

THE IMPORTANCE OF GROOVE ANALYSIS

To fully grasp a groove and absorb its ideas, it's crucial to conduct a harmonic and rhythmic analysis. This process will aid in understanding the building blocks and construction of the groove.

The harmonic analysis focuses on the function of the notes in relation to the harmony (or the chord), while the rhythmic analysis decodes the rhythmic patterns used to construct the bass line.

The harmonic and rhythmic analysis of the grooves we will play will help reinforce your learning and fully absorb the ideas. As a result of this practice, your musical vocabulary and creativity will expand.

This analysis will become the standard practice from this lesson forward, and we will analyze all the grooves we play. In the beginning, it might seem a bit daunting, but rest assured that by the end of the book, you will be able to do it in seconds!

To facilitate the description of the analysis, we'll use the following abbreviations:

Rhythmic pattern: **RP**
Chromatic pattern: **CP**
Measure: **M**
Beat: **B**

Above the staff are indicated the rhythmic patterns.
Beneath the notes are the numbers that indicate the function of the notes as either chord tones or passing notes.
Chromatic notes will be indicated by **Chr**.

Let's do our first analysis of example 4.5.

Analysis of example 4.5

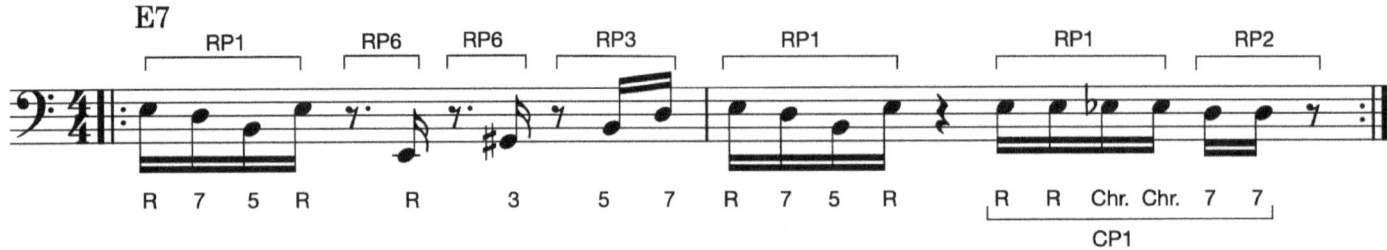

Harmonic analysis:

The grove is in E7, and all the notes are from the E7 arpeggio, root, 3rd, 5th, and 7th (E, G♯, B, and D) except the Eb in the second measure.

In this case, the E♭ is a chromatic note between the root (E) and the minor 7th (D) of the chord, CP1: M2-B3 (It states that chromatic pattern 1 is used in measure 2 on beat 3).

Rhythmic analysis:

RP1: M1-B1, M2-B1, M2-B3 (It states that rhytmic pattern 1 is used in measure 1 on beat 3, etc.).
RP2: M2-B4
RP3: M1-B4
RP6: M1-B2, M1-B3

After the analysis, you should now comprehend every note related to the harmony and its rhythmic patterns. If you have difficulties playing the rhythms, you can now isolate which rhythmic pattern needs additional practice.

See below the example of how to practice the rhythmic patterns of Example 4.5.

 ## Example 4.6: Rhythmic Patterns Practice of Example 4.5

Practicing the groove with a single note helps to absorb the rhythm correctly before adding the complexity of the remaining notes.

With the new rhythmic pattern 6, we can create interesting variations by adding the downbeat first, see the next example.

▶ Example 4.7: Rhythmic Pattern 7

Remember: The crucial aspect is to practice slowly and precisely with the backing track or a metronome. The sense of tempo for a bass player is non-negotiable!

As you may have observed, a note was added to the downbeat, providing an interesting feel to the pattern. The duration of the first note is not crucial because we maintain the same percussive rhythm but with sustained notes.

The pattern below is an example of it, with a dotted eighth note and a sixteenth note.

▶ Example 4.8: Rhythmic Pattern 8

Note: This pattern has the exact rhythmic attacks as pattern 7, with the first note sustained until the next attack.

If you have mastered pattern 6, patterns 7 and 8 should not be too difficult.

The final rhythmic patterns in this lesson are a combination of two patterns we have already learned, RP 2 and RP6.

▶ Example 4.9: Rhythmic Pattern 9

Example 4.10 is a similar pattern, with the second note sustained (held longer).

▶ Example 4.10: Rhythmic Pattern 10

Let's put in practice these new rhythms in the next groove.

▶ Example 4.11: Groove with Rhythmic Patterns 9 and 10

Analysis of example 4.11

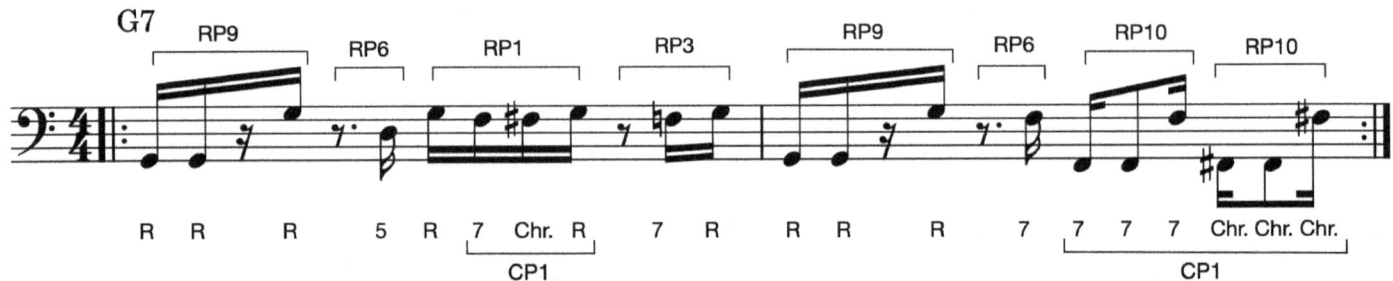

Harmonic analysis:

The notes are the root, 5th, 7th, of G7 arpeggio (G, D, F) except the chromatic passing note F♯ part of CP1: M1-B3, M2-B4

It is worth noting that the CP1 in measure two is used over two beats. The passing note does not have to resolve immediately like in measure one, but as in this case, it can last a full beat.

Rhythmic Analysis:

You should be able by now to spot the rhythmic patterns easily.

RP1: M1-B3
RP3: M1-B4
RP6: M1-B2, M2-B2
RP9: M1-B1, M2-B1
RP10: M2-B3/B4

SUMMARY

- **The fourth 16th note in a beat has opened new and interesting rhythmic configurations that enrich the grooves.**

- **We added five new rhythmic patterns to our vocabulary to practice.**

- **The rhythmic and harmonic analysis of the grooves will be the default practice as it is one of the best techniques to help understand and learn new concepts and grooves.**

LESSON

Objectives

- **The Perfect 4th**
- **Chromatic Pattern 2**
- **Playing Techniques: Finger-Style**

5

THE PERFECT 4TH

In Lesson 3, we discovered that the dominant 7th is the most frequently used chord in funk music. To craft bass lines, we have utilized the chord tones along with the chromatic passing note between the 7th and the root (CP1) so far.

In this lesson, we will introduce the first non-chord tone: the perfect 4th, as an available note to create our lines. However, the perfect 4th does have limitations as it tends to clash with the major 3rd. Therefore, it is primarily used as a passing note—a note whose main function is to connect two other notes.

Below is the C7 chord with the perfect 4th (indicated by a diamond note head) added to the arpeggio. In this instance, the 4th serves to connect the 3rd and the 5th.

▶ Example 5.1: Perfect 4ᵗʰ in the Dominant Chord

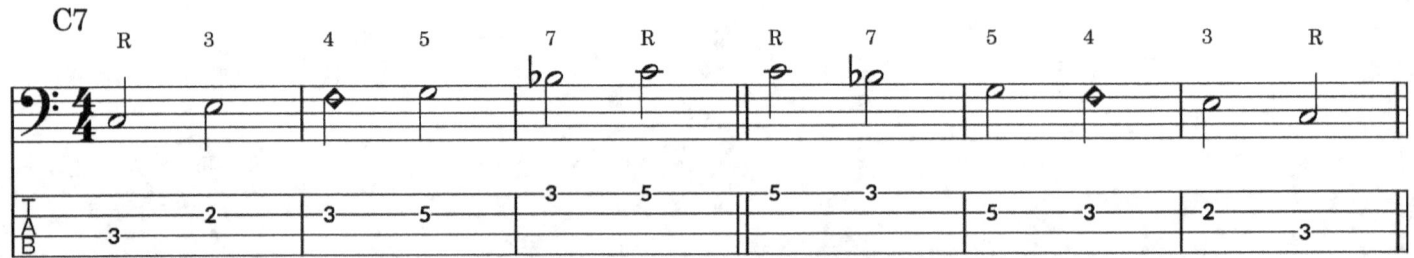

Let's see and hear the 4th in a groove — pay attention to how it functions as a passing note.

▶ Example 5.2: Groove with the 4th as a Passing Note

Analysis of example 5.2

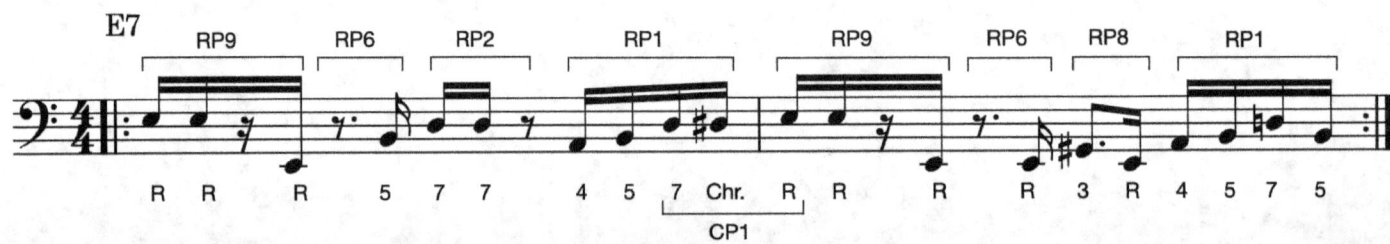

Harmonic analysis:

The groove is centered around the E7 chord, using the root, 3rd, 5th, and 7th (E, G♯, B, D), with the 4th (A) as a passing note between the 3rd and the 5th. Additionally, the chromatic note D♯ serves as a passing note between the 7th and the root (CP1: M1-B4).

Rhythmic analysis:

All the rhythms are from our vocabulary:

RP1: M1-B4, M2-B4
RP2: M1-B3
RP6: M1-B2, M2-B2
RP8: M2-B3
RP9: M1-B1, M2-B2

 Example 5.3: Chromatic Pattern 2

Understanding the use of the perfect 4th in a dominant 7th chord paves the way for introducing the chromatic tone (CP2) between the 4th and the 5th, both ascending and descending (indicated by a diamond note head), ♯4 and ♭5.

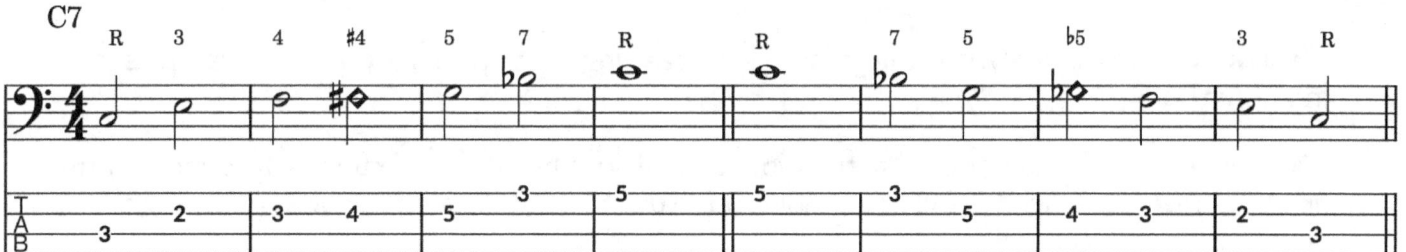

Tip: In Example 5.3, we encounter the same note with different names. In measure 2, the F♯ is ascending, and in measure 7, the note is descending and is written as G♭.

When notes appear like this, they are called enharmonic notes, meaning they are "equivalent". "Enharmonic" is a term that can also be used to describe chords and key signatures written in a similar fashion (e.g., F♯7 and G♭7).

Let's see and listen CP2 in a groove.

 Example 5.4: Groove with Chromatic Pattern 2

Analysis of example 5.4

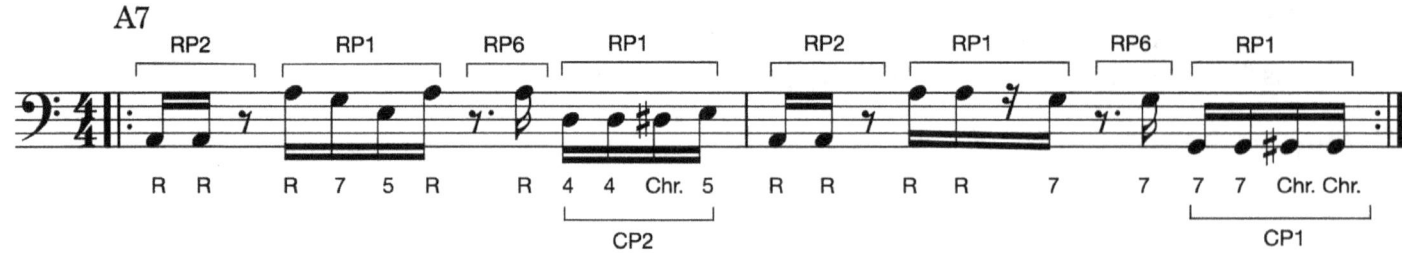

Harmonic Analysis:

The groove uses the Root, 5th, and 7th of the A7 chord (A, E, and G) plus the 4th (D).

The chromatic passing note D♯, between the 4th (D) and the 5th (E), is CP2: M1-B4.
The G♯ between the 7th (G) and the root (A), is CP1: M2-B4.

Rhythmic analysis:

RP1: M1-B2/B4, M2-B4
RP2: M1-B1, M2-B1
RP6: M1-B3, M2-B3
RP9: M2-B2

Remember: We will analyze all the grooves, emphasizing the patterns used in the examples to reinforce our learning.

Over time and with consistent practice, you will develop the ability to effortlessly identify patterns in any groove you play. This skill will enable you to use them spontaneously when creating or improvising new funk grooves!

Note: If you're familiar with the Blues scale (no worries if you're not; we'll cover it in later lessons), you might wonder why we consider the ♯4/♭5 of CP2 only as a passing note and not part of the Blues scale. The ♯4 is, in indeed, one of the crucial 'blue' notes of the Blues scale, but the way it is used in the previous groove, it sounds like a chromatic passing note and less 'bluesy.'

As we progress through the lessons, we will delve into the nuances of the Blues scale, an essentiual sound for creating bass lines. Be patient; we still have some ground to cover before then!

Now, let's play a few more lines with CP2.

▶ Example 5.5: Groove with Chromatic Pattern 2

Analysis of Example 5.5

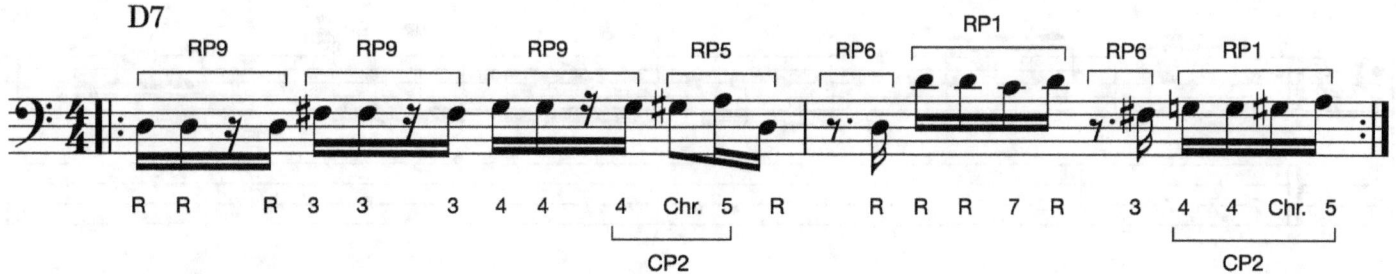

Harmonic Analysis:

All the notes of the D7 arpeggio are used in this groove (D, F♯, A, C), plus the 4th (G).
The chromatic note G♯ is used between the 4th and the 5th of the chord,
denoted as CP2: M1-B4, M2-B4.

Note that the F♯ is not a chromatic note; it is the 3rd of the chord.

Rhythmic Analysis:

RP1: M2-B2/B4
RP5: M1-B4
RP6: M2-B1/B3
RP9: M1-B1/B2/B3

In this groove, we have the example of connecting the 3rd and the 5th of the chord with the 4th and the ♯4.
This is quite a common use of this passing note, and we will see it more and more as we progress through the lessons.

PLAYING TECHNIQUES: FINGER-STYLE SOUND

This lesson also introduces a new topic, playing techniques.

Various techniques are employed in funk bass, including finger-style, hammered on and off notes, muted notes, and double stops. Our initial focus will be on finger-style playing.

Finger-style refers to the tone's sound of the bass lines you produce.

You have a palette of tones at your disposal, ranging from warm and round sounds to more precise and defined percussive ones.

The placement of your right hand on the bass determines these sounds. Placing your hand on the pickup close to the neck creates a rounder sound, while positioning it closer to the bridge produces a more defined sound.

Both sounds are excellent and can be utilized in different contexts; it depends on the style you want to convey in the tunes you are playing.

Let's hear the same line played with these two sounds.

▶ Example 5.6: Groove with a "Defined" Sound

Analysis of Example 5.6

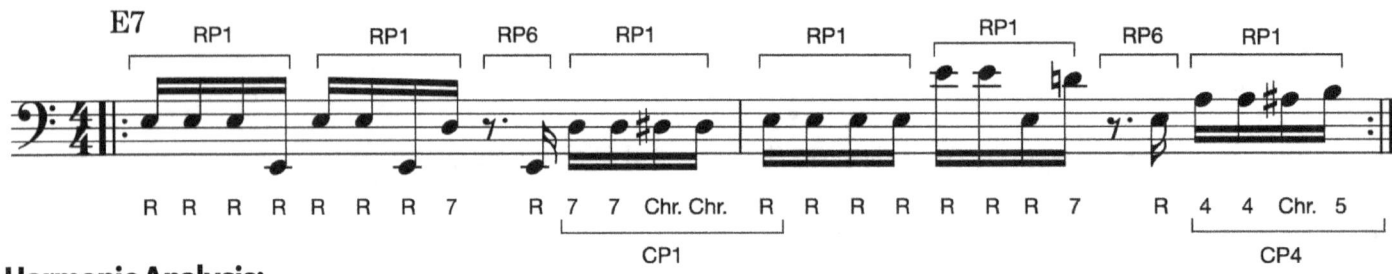

Harmonic Analysis:

The chord tones used in the groove are the root, 5th, and 7th of the E7 chord (E, B, and D), we also use the 4th (A) and two chromatic notes, D♯ and A♯.
The D♯ is the passing note between the 7th and the root, CP1: M1-B4.
The A♯ is the passing note between the 4th (A) and the 5th (B), CP2: M2-B4.

Rhythmic Analysis:

RP1:   M1-B1/B2/B4, M2-B1/B2/B4
RP6:   M1-B3, M2-B3

▶ Example 5.7: Groove with a "Round" Sound

Same groove as in Example 5.6 played with a different technique.

Bass players familiar with Jaco Pastorius and Francis Rocco Prestia are familiar with these distinctive sounds and styles. These legendary bass players had different styles: Prestia preferred to use the "round" sound, while Pastorius mostly used the "defined" sound in his funk lines. Although they had opposite styles, they both produced compelling funk lines. To become more familiar with the feel of playing in a different area of the strings, try to use both styles when you learn a new groove.

SUMMARY

- **The perfect 4th allows you to use new and interesting musical combinations, even though it is mainly used as a passing tone between the 3rd and the 5th.**

- **We can use another chromatic passing note between the 4th and the 5th, the CP2.**

- **Introduction of our first playing technique: Finger-style. Now you can choose what type of sound you want to give to bass lines.**

LESSON

6

OBJECTIVES

- **The second 16th in a beat**
- **Four new rhythmic patterns**
- **Application of the new rhythmic patterns in grooves**

The Second 16th in a Beat

We finally learn the latest rhythmic 16th attack in a beat - the second 16th note in a beat!

With this, we reach the full potential of the possible rhythmic combinations available to create a funk line.

Let's do a quick recap. In the previous lessons, we learned the rhythmic patterns that start with the downbeat, upbeat and the fourth 16th of the four available notes in a beat.

Example 6.1: 16th Notes on the downbeat, upbeat, and third beat

We've practiced and analyzed nine rhythmic patterns within grooves, incorporating rhythmic exercises to facilitate a natural execution. Consistent and creative practice is key to reinforcing your learning.

In this lesson, we're approaching the completion of mastering all possible rhythmic permutations, equipping you to create captivating funk bass lines.

Example 6.2: The Second 16th Note in a Beat

As in the fourth 16th note in lesson 4, we will do preliminary exercises with the same foot-tapping technique to help play this rhythm precisely.

1. We will play the whole example with pattern 2 (all 16th notes are played) and accent the second 16th.

▶ Example 6.3: Accented Second 16th note in RP1

2. We slowly decrease the volume of the first note until only the second 16th can be heard, which becomes our new rhythmic pattern.

▶ Example 6.4: Rhythmic Pattern 11

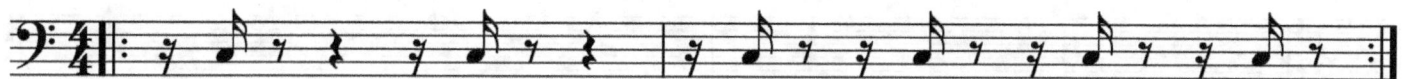

We have now learned all the note attacks in a beat and can play any rhythm - this is a significant achievement!

Let's practice with a groove that focuses on the new rhythmic pattern.

▶ Example 6.5: Groove with Rhythmic Pattern 11

Analysis of example 6.5

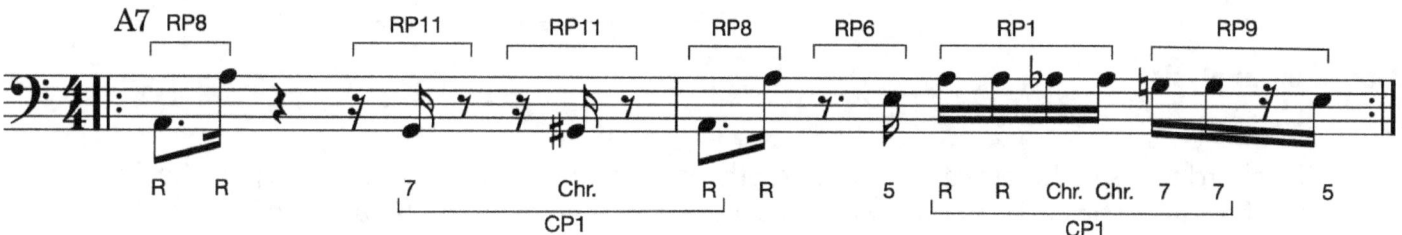

Harmonic analysis

The notes of this groove are the root, 5th, and 7th of the A7 chord (A, E, G), plus the chromatic passing note G♯/A♭ in measures 1 and 2 between the root (A) and the 7th of the chord (G), CP1: M1-B4, M2-B3 (ascending and descending).

Rhythmic analysis

RP1: M2-B3
RP6: M2-B2
RP8: M1-B1, M2-B1
RP9: M2-B4
RP11: M1-B3/B4

Let's continue building on the remaining patterns with this rhythmic attack.

▶ Example 6.6: Rhythmic Pattern 12

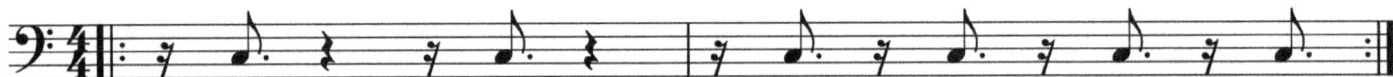

This is a straightforward pattern, much like the one we just learned, however, this one has a sustained note instead of a short one.

▶ Example 6.7: Groove with Rhythmic Pattern 12

Analysis of example 6.7

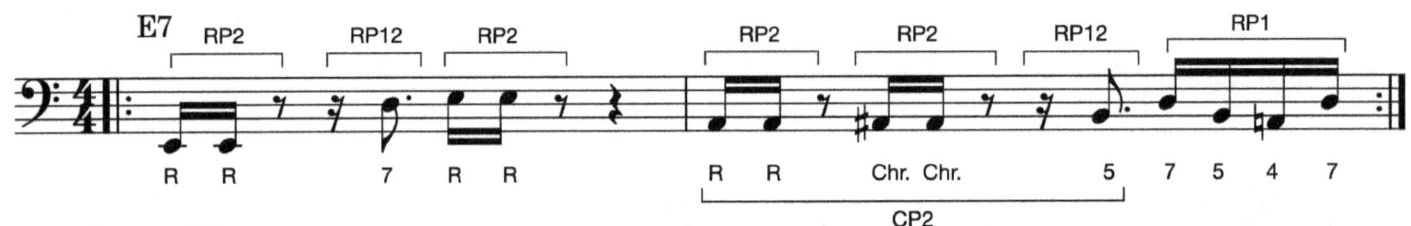

Harmonic analysis

The chord tones in this grove are the root, 5th, and 7th of the E7 chord (E, B, D), plus the 4th (A), and the chromatic passing note A♯ in measure two, between the 4th (A) and the 5th (B), CP2: M2–B2.

Rhythmic analysis

RP1:   M2–B4
RP2:   M1–B1/B3, M2–B1/B2
RP12: M1–B2, M2–B3

The following pattern is a combination of patterns 11 and 3.

▶ Example 6.8: Rhythmic Pattern 12

This is a very used pattern that will make the grooves even funkier!

▶ Example 6.9: Groove with Rhythmic Pattern 13

Analysis of example 6.9

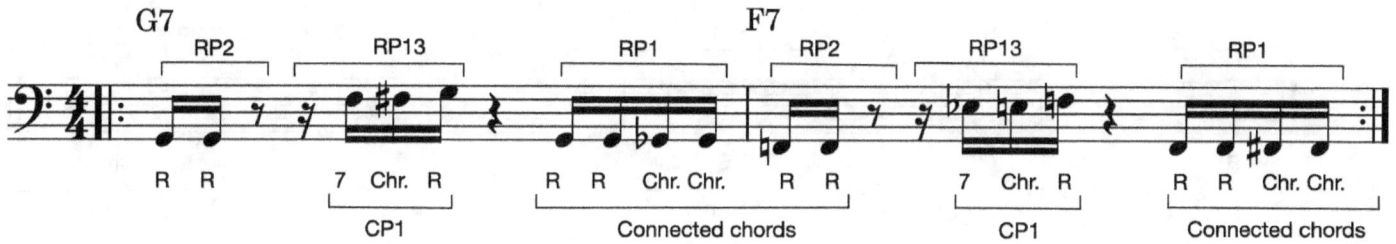

Harmonic analysis

The chord tones of this groove are the root and 7th of the G7 (G, F) and F7 (F, E♭) chords.

There are two chromatic passing notes, F♯ in measure one CP1: M1-B2 in G7, and E natural in measure two CP1: M2-B2

The G♭/F♯ at the end of measures 1 and 2 is not a chromatic pattern because it doesn't connect chord tones but is a chromatic passing note between F7 and G7. We will discuss connecting chords chromatically in more detail later on.

Rhythmic analysis

RP1: M1-B4, M2-B4
RP2: M1-B1, M2-B2
RP13: M1-B2, M2-B2

Finally, we have our last pattern made up of patterns 6 and 11

▶ Example 6.10: Rhythmic Pattern 14

Tip: If you find this challenging, apply the technique we used to learn pattern 11 (along with foot tapping) to internalize the rhythmic pulse.

Now let's apply the three rhythmic patterns into a single groove.

▶ Example 6.11: Groove with Rhythmic Pattern 14

Analysis of example 6.11

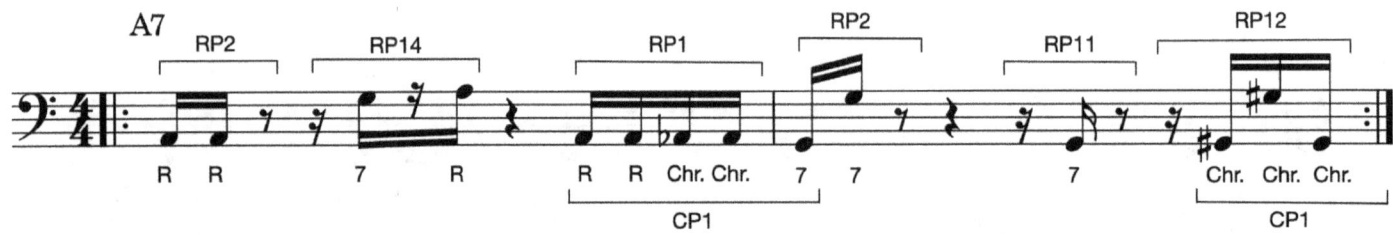

Harmonic analysis

The chord tones of this groove are the root and 7th of the A7 chord (A, G).
The chromatic passing note A♭/G♯ is used in both measures between the root and the 7th.
In both cases, we analyze it as CP1: M1-B4, M2-B4.

Rhythmic analysis

RP1: M1-B4   RP12: M2-B4
RP2: M1-B1, M2-B1   RP14: M1-B2
RP11: M2-B3

Using a simple, harmonic line that includes different rhythmic patterns can make the line sound quite funky!
Mastering rhythmic patterns is key to creativity!

SUMMARY

- **With the rhythmic attack on the second 16th on a beat, we added four new rhythmic patterns and have almost mastered all the available patterns.**

- **Simple 2 or 3 notes bass lines can become quite funky with the application and mixed use of the rhythmic patterns.**

- **Additional rhythmic practice with the exercises in the appendix will help you absorb and master the new rhythmic patterns.**

LESSON

7

THE MAJOR 6TH

The major 6th is a new sound to add to our bass lines. It differs from the 4th because we can play it freely with other chord tones (not only as a passing note) without worrying about unwanted dissonances.

Below you will see the major 6th (diamond note head) added to the note set, arpeggio plus the 4th

▶ Example 7.1: Major 6th in the C7 Chord

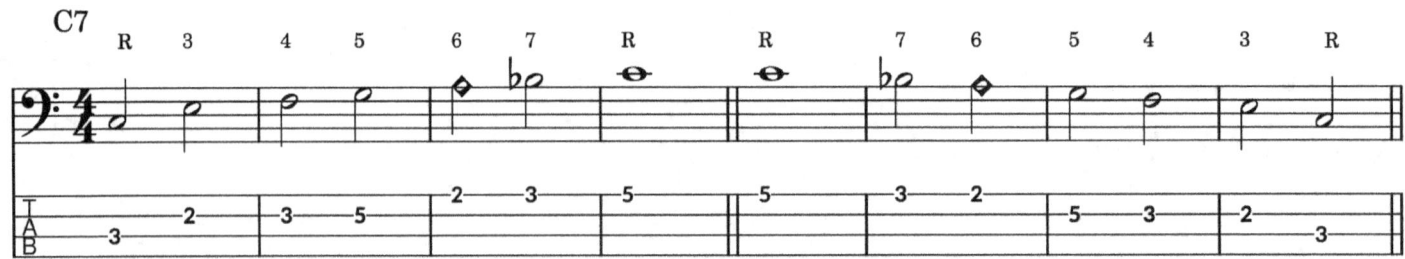

Tip: In music theory, the notes between the chord tones, the 2nd, 4th, and 6th, are called "extensions" and are usually called 9th, 11th, and 13th.

For simplicity, we will refer to those intervals as 2nd, 4th, and 6th.

Here is another example with the major 6th, this time in E7.

▶ Example 7.2: Major 6th in the E7 Dominant Chord

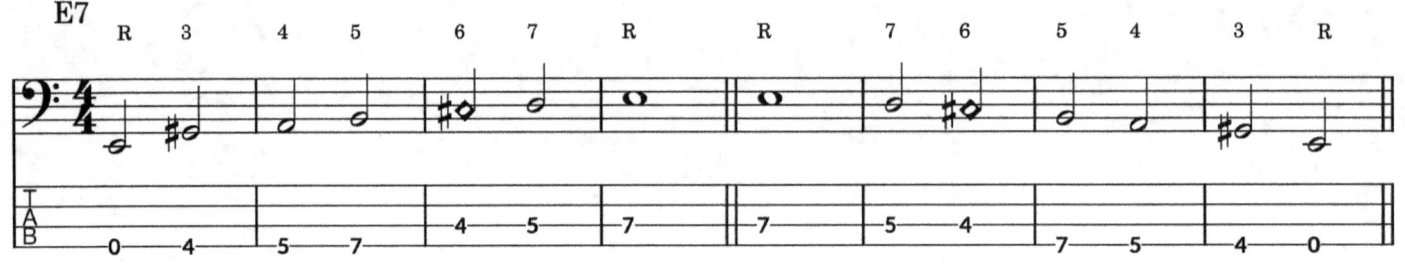

The 6th sounds pretty good mixed with the 7th, let's hear it in the next groove.

▶ Example 7.3: Groove with the Major 6th

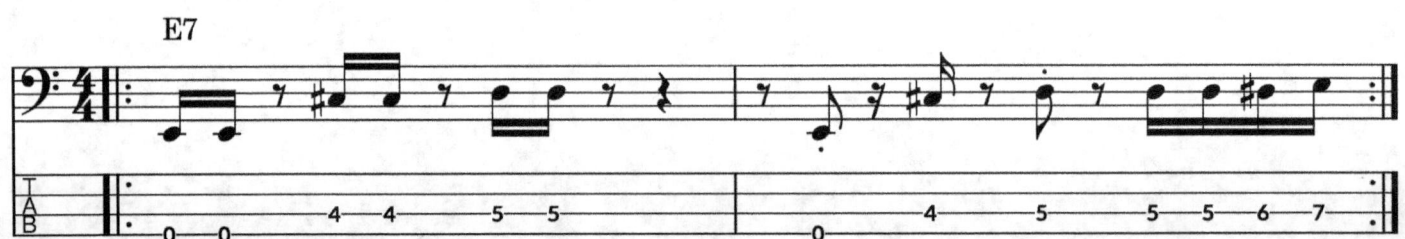

Analysis of example 7.3

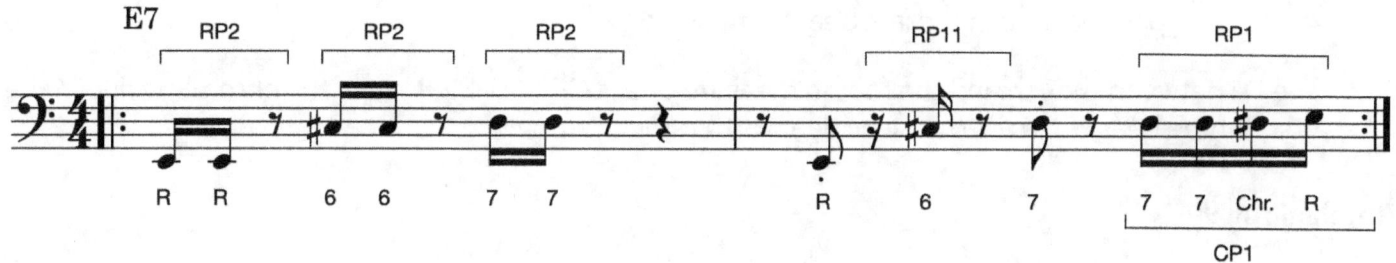

Harmonic analysis

The chord tones in this groove are the root and 7th of the E7 chord (E, D), the C♯ is the major 6th.

In the last beat of the second measure, there is a chromatic passing note D♯ between the 7th and the root, which is CP1: M2-B4.

Rhythmic analysis

RP1:   M2-B4
RP2:   M1-B1/B2/B3
RP11: M2-B2

In M2-B1/B3, we play a short upbeat, so it is not marked as RP.

(In case you need a quick refresh on the upbeats, go to lesson 2, example 2.1.)

Now that we are familiar with the sound of the major 6th, we can combine CP1 to obtain an interesting chromatic line.

▶ Example 7.4: Groove with CP1 Combined with the Major 6th

Analysis of example 7.4

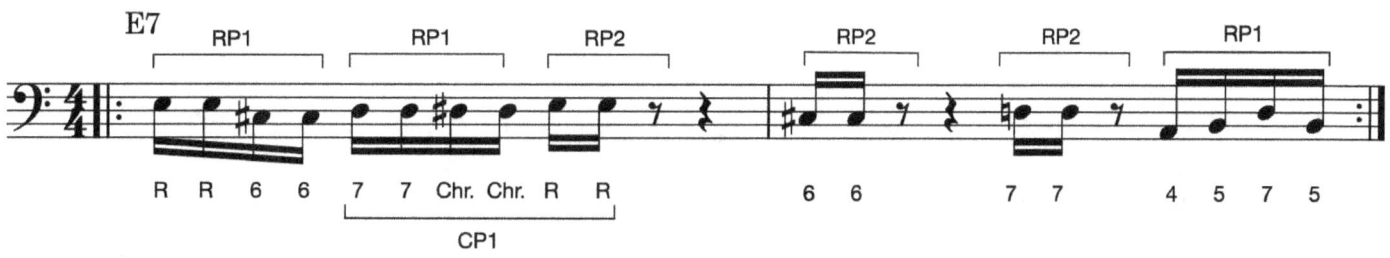

Harmonic analysis

The chord tones used in this groove are the root, 5th, and 7th of the E7 chord (E, B, D). We use the 4th (A) as a passing note in the last beat of measure two.

The D♯ between the 7th and the root in measure one is CP1: M1-B2. Notice the chromatic line in the first 3 three beats - this is a musical idea worth remembering!

Rhythmic analysis

RP1: M1-B1/B2, M2-B4
RP2: M1-B3, M2-B2/B3

CHROMATIC PATTERN 3

With the major 6th, we can now create chromaticism between the 5th and the 6th.
Chromatic Pattern 3 (CP3) uses the 5th of the arpeggio plus the ♯5th or ♭6th (diamond note head).

▶ Example 7.5: Chromatic Pattern 3

Compared to the first two chromatic patterns, CP3 is not quite as common, but you can still create interesting bass lines, as in the example below.

▶ Example 7.6: Groove with CP3 and CP1 in C7

In the video, note how I play the B♭ on two different points of the fingerboard. This is to facilitate the execution of the groove.

Tip: Try to find the most comfortable fingering to play a groove whenever possible. In the track above, I played the line with the 'closed' position of the hand, with only the first, second, and fourth fingers to keep my hand relaxed the entire time.

Analysis of example 7.6

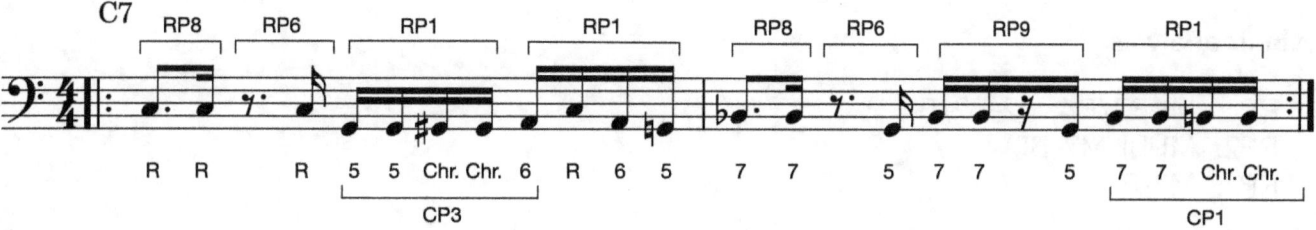

Harmonic analysis

The chord tones used in this groove are the Root, 5th, and 7th of the C7 chord (C, G, B♭) and the 6th (A) in the last beat of measure one.

In measure one, the G♯ between the 5th (G) and the 6th (A) is the new CP3: M1-B3.
The B natural at the end of measure two between the 7th and the Root is CP1: M2-B4.

Rhythmic analysis

RP1: M1-B3/B4, M2-B4
RP6: M1-B2, M2-B2
RP8: M1-B1, M2-B1
RP9: M2-B3

Let's practice the major 6th and CP3 in A7.

▶ Example 7.7: Groove with CP3 and CP1 in A7

We use the open A string to play this line.

Analysis of example 7.7

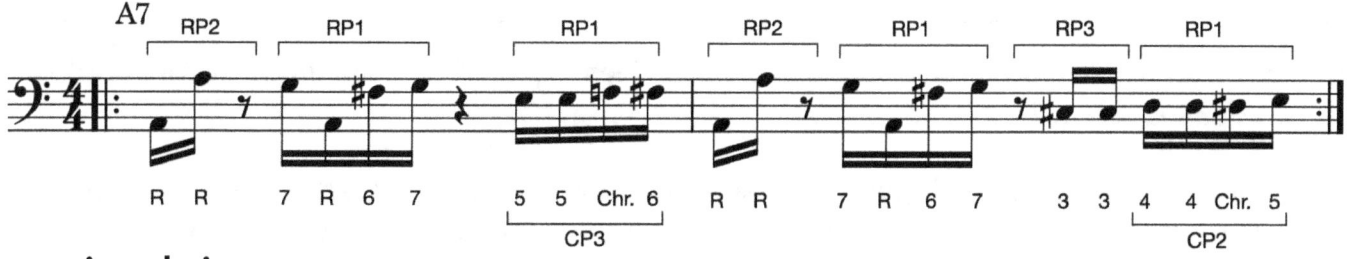

Harmonic analysis

In this groove, we use all of the chord tones of the A7 chord (A, C♯, E, G). We also use the 6th (F♯) in measures one and two, and the 4th (D) at the end of measure two.

The first chromatic pattern uses the F natural between the 5th (E) and the 6th (F♯), CP3: M1-B4. The second one includes the D♯ between the 4th (D) and the 5th (E), CP2 M2:B4.

Rhythmic analysis

RP1:   M1-B2/B4, M2-B2/B4
RP2:   M1-B1, M2-B1
RP3:   M2-B3

PLAYING TECHNIQUES: HAMMER-ON AND PULL-OFF

Hammer-on and pull-off technique is used to produce the sound of a note without plucking the string but by hammering on the fingers or pulling them off.

It's essential to develop strength in the fingers to hammer-on the notes before applying it to grooves. Let's try the following exercise.

▶ **Example 7.8: Hammer-On and Pull-Off on the A String**

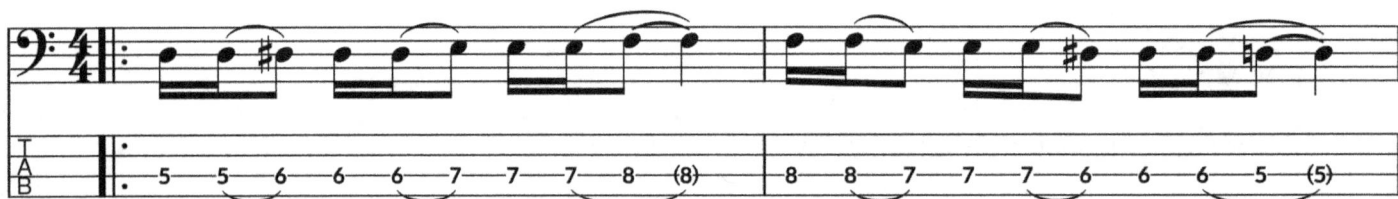

▶ **Example 7.9: Hammer-On and Pull-Off on the G String**

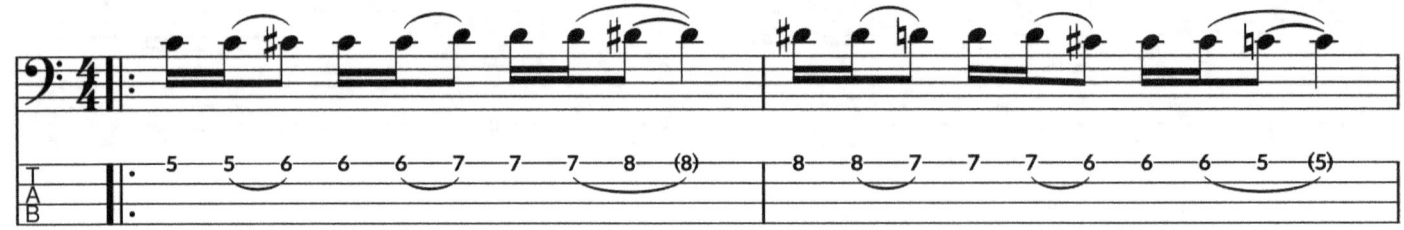

SUMMARY

- **The major 6th is a great sound to add to our bass lines, especially in combination with the 7th of the dominant chord.**

- **With the major 6th at our disposal there are more possibilities to create chromaticism between the 5th and the 6th (that is CP3), and we can combine it with other chromatic patterns.**

- **Hammer-on and pull-off is a good technique we will use to create even more interesting bass lines. For the moment, focus on practicing the technique building exercise on all the strings.**

LESSON

OBJECTIVES

- **Hammer-on and pull-off grooves**
- **Final rhythmic patterns**
- **Playing Technique: Muted notes**

8

HAMMER-ON AND PULL-OFF GROOVES

Now that you've learned the hammer-on and pull-off technique, let's practice it with some grooves.

▶ Example 8.1: E7 Groove with Hammer-Ons and Pull-Offs

Analysis of example 8.1

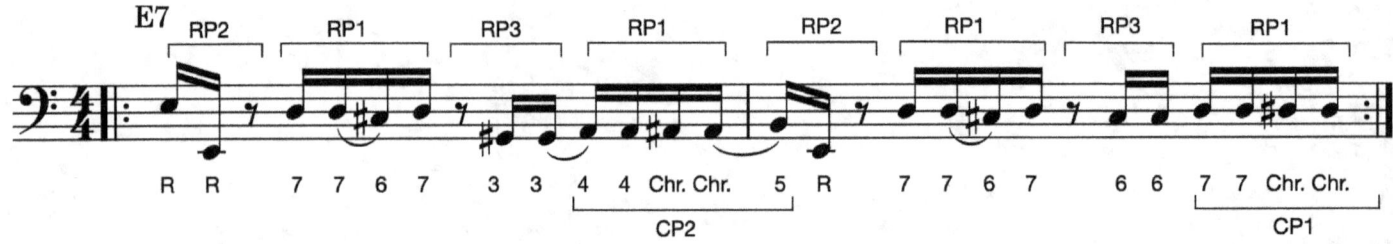

Harmonic analysis

In this line, we use all of the E7 chord tones (E, G♯, B, D), plus the 6th (C♯) and the 4th (A). We also include two chromatic passing notes, A♯ from the 4th (A) to the 5th (B), this is CP2: M1-B4, and the second one, D♯, connecting the 7th (D) to the root of the chord (E), CP1: M2-B4.

Rhythmic analysis

RP1: M1-B2/B4, M2-B2/B4
RP2: M1-B1, M2-B1
RP3: M1-B3, M2-B3

Tip: If you have difficulties playing this groove, play it first without any hammer-ons or pull-offs, then, once you are confident with it, add the hammered notes one at a time until you are ready to add the others.

▶ Example 8.2: G7 Groove with Hammer-ons and Pull-Offs

Analysis of example 8.2

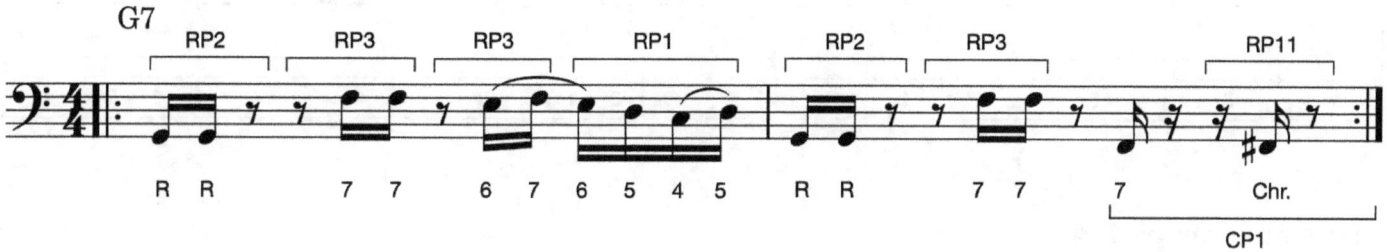

Harmonic analysis

This line uses the root and the 7th of the G7 chord (G, F) plus the 6th (E) and the 4th (C).

F♯ is a chromatic passing note from the 7th (F) to the root (G) in the last beat of measure two, CP1: M2-B4.

Rhythmic analysis

RP1: M1-B4
RP2: M1-B1, M2-B1
RP3: M1-B2/B3, M2-B2
RP11: M2-B4

Note that in M2-B3, we play a short upbeat and are not marked as RP.

This playing technique gives a different sound to this groove and can be used freely on any groove.

THE FINAL RHYTHMIC PATTERNS

Believe it or not, we have reached the last of the rhythmic patterns to use at our disposal! They are variations of the patterns from lesson 6.

▶ Example 8.3: Rhythmic Pattern 15

This is quite a dynamic rhythm, as seen in the next groove.

▶ Example 8.4: Groove with Rhythmic Pattern 15

Analysis of example 8.4

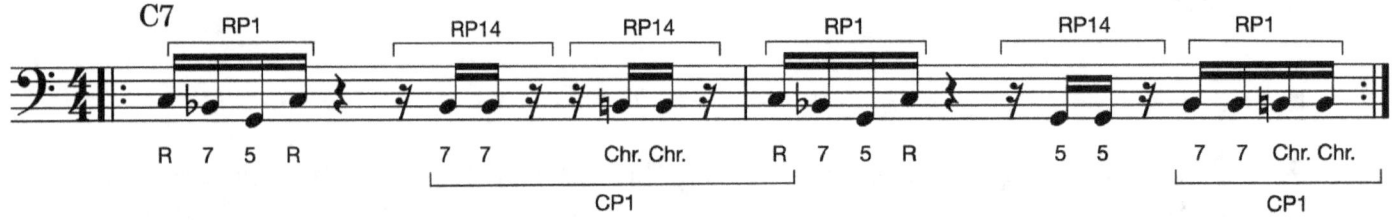

Harmonic analysis

In this groove, we use the root, 5th, and the 7th of the C7 chord (C, G, B♭).

The B natural is a chromatic passing note from the 7th (B♭) to the root (C) in the last beat of measure one and two, making this CP1: M1-B3, M2-B4.

Rhythmic analysis

RP1:   M1-B1, M2-B2/B4
RP14: M1-B3/B4, M2-B3

▶ Example 8.5: Rhythmic Pattern 16

In this variation, the second note is held until the next beat.

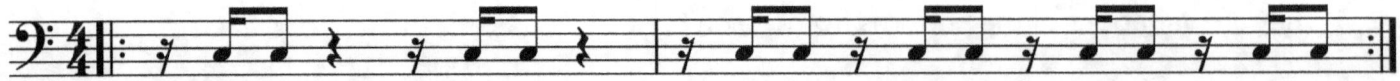

Let's hear it in practice.

▶ Example 8.6: Groove with Rhythmic Pattern 16

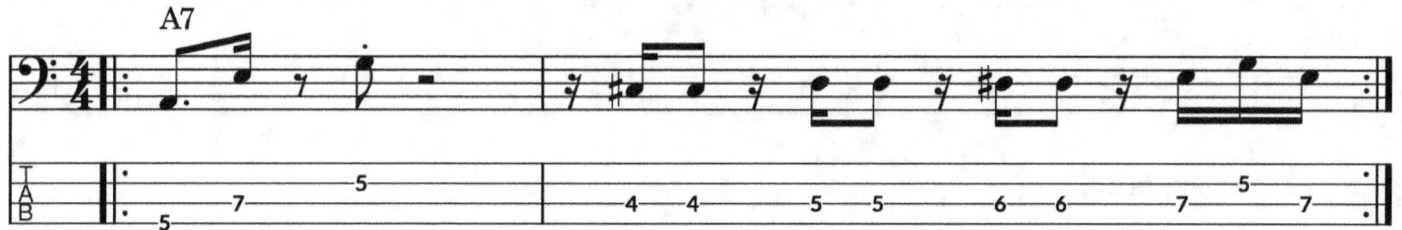

Analysis of example 8.6

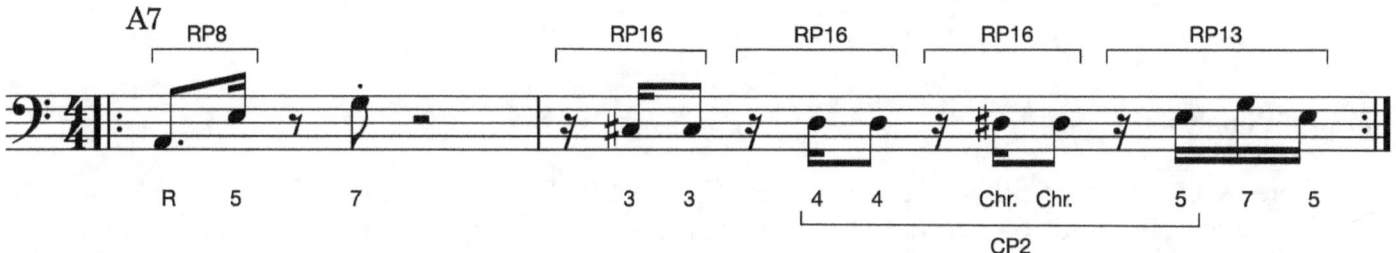

Harmonic analysis

We use all of the chord tones of the A7 chord (A, C♯, E, G) with the 4th (D) as a passing note. The D♯ is the chromatic passing note between the 4th and the 5th, making this CP2: M2-B3.

Rhythmic analysis

RP8: M1-B1
RP13: M2-B4
RP16: M2-B1/B2/B3

The upbeat note in M1-B2 is not an RP.

The final rhythmic pattern in our vocabulary is a simple variation of RP2 we learned in lesson 2 that uses a sustained second note.

▶ Example 8.7: Rhythmic Pattern 17

Let's combine it with other patterns in the next grove.

Example 8.8: Groove with Rhythmic Pattern 17

Analysis of example 8.8

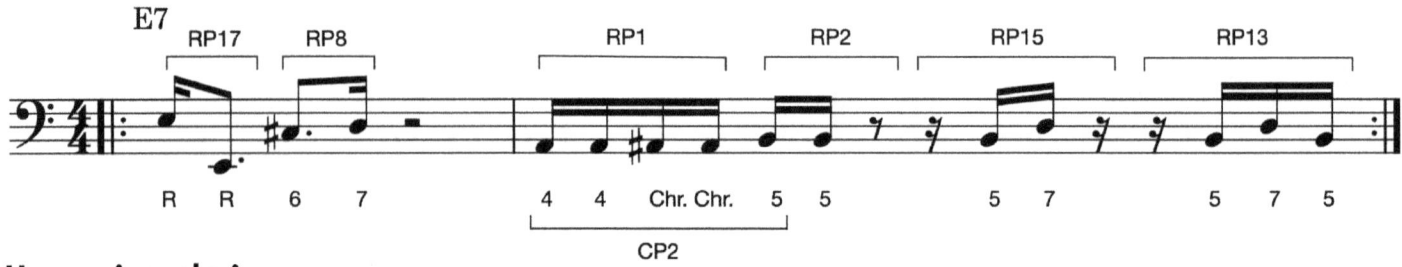

Harmonic analysis

Here we use the root, 5th, and the 7th of the E7 chord (E, B, D) plus the 6th (C♯).
The A♯ is a chromatic passing note from the 4th (A) to the 5th (B) in the first beat of measure two, making this CP2: M2-B1.

Rhythmic analysis

RP1: M2-B1	RP13: M2-B4
RP2: M2-B2	RP15: M2-B3
RP8: M1-B2	RP17: M1-B1

PLAYING TECHNIQUE: MUTED NOTES

Now that we have learned and practiced all available rhythmic patterns, we can introduce an essential technique that adds a percussive sound to bass lines: muted notes.

A muted note is a plucked note that produces a percussive effect instead of an actual tone.

There are various ways to produce this, the most common way is to pluck the string while at the same time touching the string with two or more fingers to stop making any notes.
Using only one finger will most likely produce a harmonic sound and is not what we want.

Let's practice playing muted notes with this exercise.

 Example 8.9: Muted Notes on the A String

Pay attention in the video to how I produced the first muted note after playing the first three notes. I lift my index finger but keep contact with the string while touching the string (not pressing) with the middle finger as well, having the two fingers touching the string to avoid producing the harmonic note.
The remaining muted notes are produced with the same principle, by easing the pressure but still touching the string.

Let's mute the notes on the remaining strings.

Example 8.10: Muted Notes on the D String

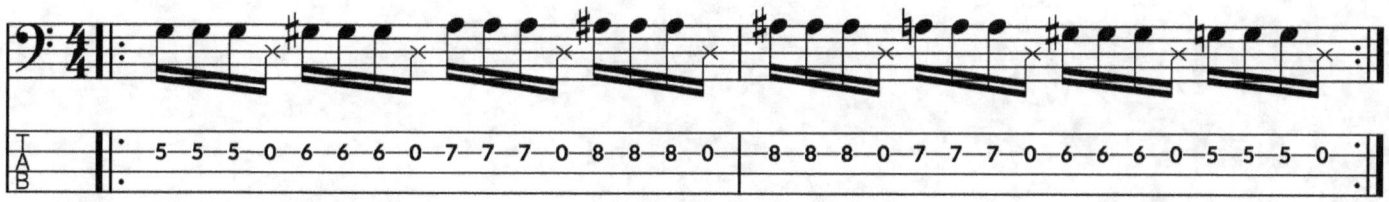

Example 8.11: Muted Notes on the G String

Example 8.12: Muted Notes on the E String

SUMMARY

- **We applied the hammer-on and pull-off technique in two grooves.**

- **Learn the last rhythmic patterns to round out our vocabulary.**

- **Learn how to play muted notes. This playing style is a great technique to add a percussive effect to bass lines.**

LESSON

OBJECTIVES

- **The Major 2nd**
- **The Mixolydian scale**
- **Muted noted grooves**

9

THE MAJOR 2ND

In this lesson, we introduce the last non-chord tone available in our vocabulary to create bass lines over a 7th chord - the major 2nd

This interval is commonly used as a passing note, especially to the 3rd of the chord.

In Example 9.1, the major 2nd (diamond note head) has been added to our note set.

Example 9.1: Major 2nd in the C7 chord

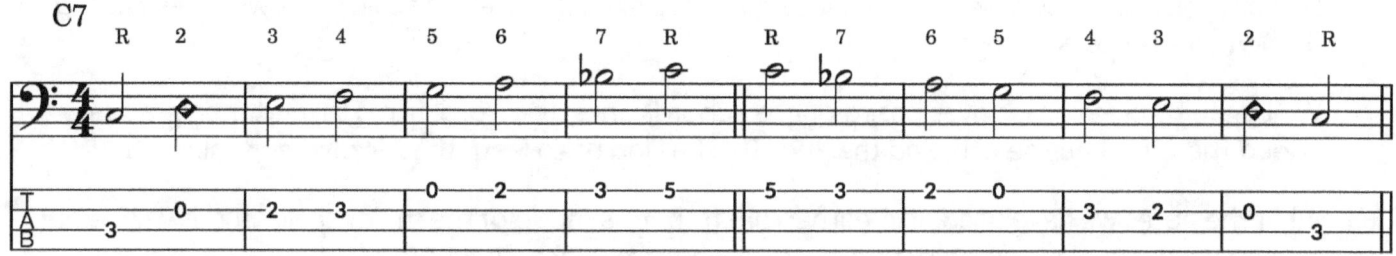

Let's practice a groove that emphasizes the 2nd.

Example 9.2: Groove Major 2nd in the C7 chord

Analysis of example 9.2

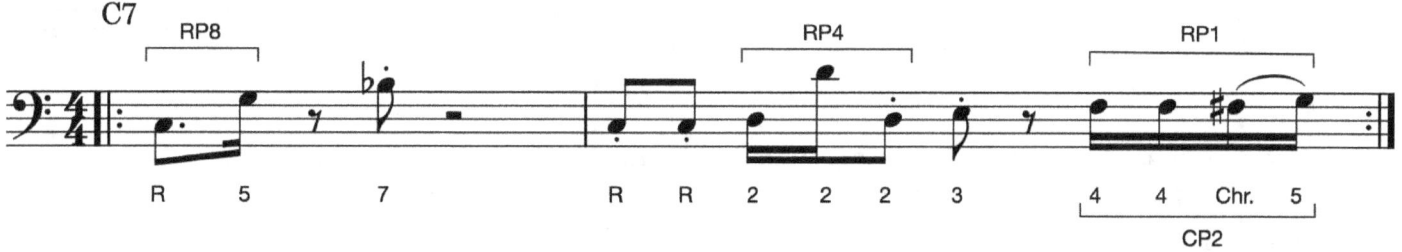

Harmonic analysis

In this groove, we use all of the chord tones of the C7 chord (C, E, G, B♭), plus the 2nd (D) and the 4th (F).

In the last beat of the second measure, there is a chromatic passing note, F♯, we use CP2: M2-B4.

Rhythmic analysis

RP1: M2-B4
RP4: M2-B2
RP8: M1-B1

With the major 2nd, we have all available notes to build a scale.

THE MIXOLYDIAN SCALE

By now, you should be able to appreciate the value of each note in a scale since we have learned all of them in the previous lessons.

We began by creating grooves based only on chord tones, root, 3rd, 5th, 7th, and then gradually added the 4th, then the 6th, and the 2nd. This has led us to learn the Mixolydian scale.

All of the notes we have used and learned are from this mode of the major scale, and it will be our reference choice of notes every time we play a groove over a 7th chord.

A mode is a reorganization of the notes of the major scale (and other scales) that fits a specific chord also derived from the same scale (e.g. C Major scale, G Mixolydian scale, and G7).

The way we learned all the notes was done on purpose to allow you to understand the importance of the chord tones as a first choice to build a groove. Every bass line should first reflect the harmony before we can add color with the remaining notes of the scale, including the chromatic tones.

▶ **Example 9.3: G Mixolydian scale**

When we practice this scale, we use a specific fingering pattern, however, it is important to know that we can find these notes across the fingerboard, especially if a groove requires a particular fingering outside the pattern.

Specific exercises to master the fingerboard are outside the scope of this book, but you should try to learn the notes outside of a single specific fingering pattern.

It is important to practice the Mixolydian scale starting from other roots, and in the next exercise, we will play two octaves of the E Mixolydian scale.

▶ Example 9.4: E Mixolydian scale, two octaves

This scale will be the reference of your available notes for 7th chords, with the addition of the chromatic patterns that we already know and the ones that we have yet to learn.

MUTED NOTE GROOVES

In the previous lesson, we practiced the muted notes, and in this lesson, we will apply them to grooves.

▶ Example 9.5: A7 groove with muted notes

This groove makes use of two techniques we learned so far, muted and hammered-on notes.

Analysis of example 9.5

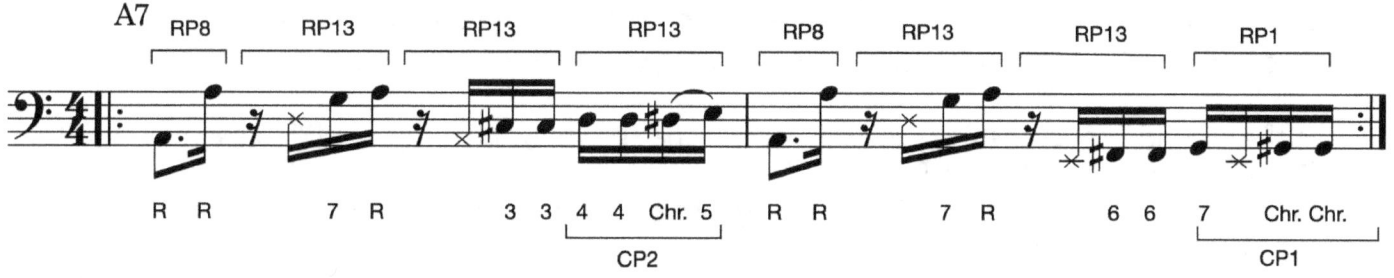

Harmonic analysis

Here we use all the chord tones of the A7 chord (A, C♯, E, G), plus the 4th (D) and the 6th (F♯).

In the fourth beat of measure one, we use the chromatic passing note D♯ between the fourth and the 5th : CP2: MI-B4.

In the fourth beat of the second measure, we use the chromatic passing note F♯ to connect the 7th (G) and the root (A): CP1: M2-B4.

Rhythmic analysis

RP1: M1-B4, M2-B4
RP8: M1-B1, M2-B1
RP13: M1-B2/B3, M2-B2/B3

Tip: If it is too difficult to play the muted notes, first, play the notes as regular notes, and once you are comfortable playing the groove, you can add the muted notes one at a time. You can do the same with the hammer-on technique.

▶ Example 9.6: E7 groove with muted notes

Analysis of example 9.6

Harmonic analysis

We use all the chord tones of the E7 chord (E, G♯, B, D), plus the 4th (A) and the 6th (C♯). This is the equivalent of saying we use the E Mixolydian scale without the 2nd.

In the second beat of the first measure, we use the chromatic passing note D♯ to connect the 7th (D) and the root (E), CP1: M2-B4.
In the fourth beat of the second measure, we use the chromatic passing note A♯ between the fourth (A) and the 5th (B), CP2: M1-B4.

Rhythmic analysis

RP1: M2-B4   RP9: M1-B1
RP6: M1-B4, M2-B3   RP14: M1-B2
RP8: M2-B1/B2

Example 9.7: G7 Groove with Muted Notes

Before playing this grove, it is a good idea to play the G Mixolydian scale to familiarize yourself with all the available notes in G7.

Analysis of example 9.7

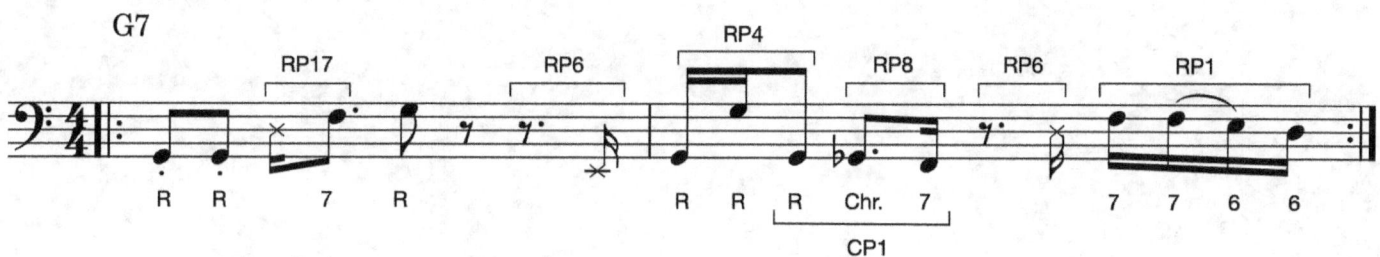

Harmonic analysis

We use the root and the 7th of the G7 chord (G, F) plus the 6th (E).

In the second beat of the second measure, we use the chromatic passing note G♭ to connect the root (G) and the 7th (F): CP1: M2-B4.

Rhythmic analysis

RP1:   M2-B4   RP8:   M2-B2
RP4:   M2-B1   RP17: M1-B2
RP6:   M1-B4, M2-B3

SUMMARY

- **We introduced the last diatonic interval to create groves on the 7th chord, the major 2nd. It is similar to the 4th as it functions mainly as a passing note between the Root and the 3rd.**

- **The Mixolydian scale is the sum of all the notes learned so far : Root, 3rd, 5th, and 7th (of the 7th chord) plus the 2nd, the 4th, and the 6th.**

- **We applied muted notes to grooves with hammer-on and off notes to create more sophisticated bass lines.**

LESSON

OBJECTIVES

- **Chromatic Pattern 4**
- **Tied rhythmic patterns**
- **Playing technique: Double stops**

CHROMATIC PATTERN 4

Now, let's expand our vocabulary with the introduction of chromatic pattern 4 (CP4). This pattern connects the 2nd to the 3rd of the 7th chord, infusing grooves with an appealing 'bluesy' sound.

Below is an example with the ♯2 or ♭3 chromatic notes.

▶ Example 10.1: Chromatic Pattern 4

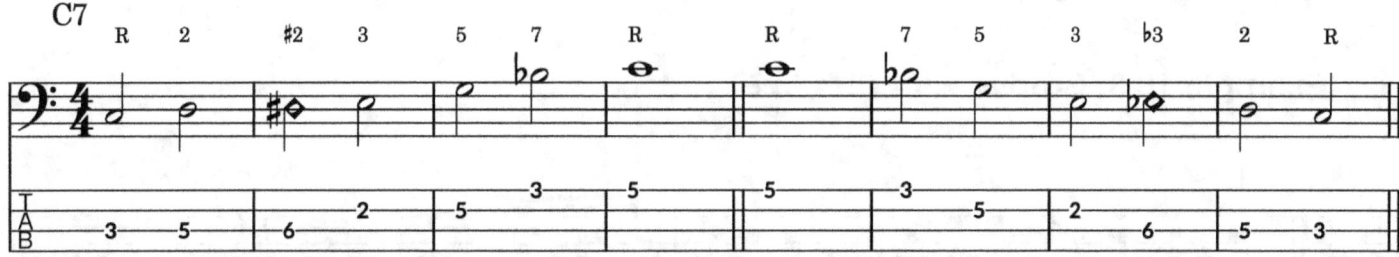

This chromatic pattern is primarily meant to be played with notes ascending, from the 2nd to the 3rd, because the approach notes tend to resolve to a chord tone, in this case, the 3rd of the 7th chord.

Let's hear the sound of this chromatic note in practice in the next grooves.

▶ Example 10.2: Groove with CP4 in C7

Analysis of Example 10.2

Harmonic analysis

We used all of the chord tones of the C7 chord (C, E, G, B♭), plus the 2nd (D) and the 6th (A).

In the second beat of the first measure, we use a chromatic passing note, D♯, between the 2nd (D) and the 3rd (E), is the new CP4: M1-B2.

Rhythmic analysis

RP1:   M2-B4
RP4:   M2-B1
RP6:   M1-B4
RP7:   M2-B2/B3
RP13: M1-B2

Let's now practice CP4 in E7.

▶ Example 10.3: Groove with CP4 in E7

Analysis of Example 10.3

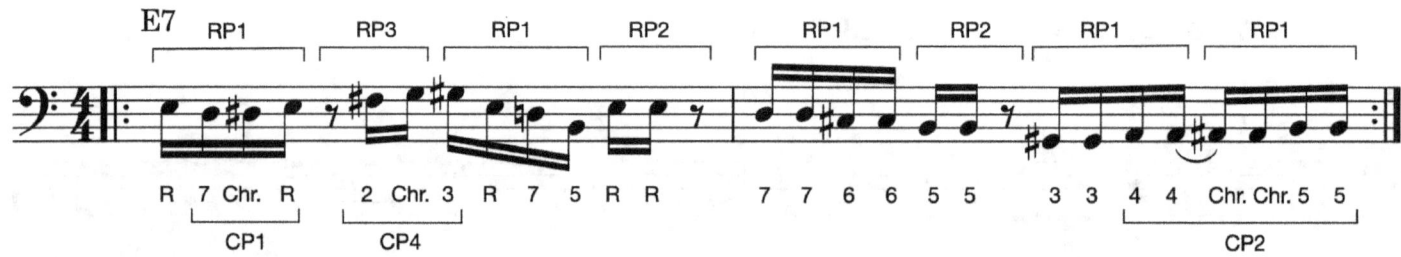

Harmonic analysis

All of the notes of the E Mixolydian scale are used in the E7 chord (E, G♯, B, D), plus the 2nd (F♯), the 4th (A), and the 6th (C♯).

In the first beat of the first measure, D♯ is used as a chromatic passing note between the 7th (D) and the Root (E), CP1: M1-B1.
In the second beat of the first measure, G is the chromatic passing note between the 2nd (F♯) and the 3rd (G♯), CP4: M1-B2.
In the last beat of measure two, A♯ is a chromatic passing note between the 4th (A) and the 5th (B), CP2: M2-B4.

Rhythmic analysis

RP1:   M1-B1/B3, M2-B1/B2/B3
RP2:   M1-B4, M2-B2
RP3:   M1-B2

TIED RHYTHMIC PATTERNS

There are occasions when a bass line has tied rhythmic patterns that might look challenging to play. Below is a simple procedure to simplify and easily play these types of lines.

Example 10.4: Groove with Tied Rhythmic Patterns

To learn this line, it will be best to simplify it to the basic rhythmic patterns by removing the ties and playing each note short. The result will be the same groove but with the familiar rhythmic patterns like the one below.

Example 10.5: Groove with Untied Rhythmic Patterns

Now that we can play this simplified line, we need only to let the notes ring as in the original example, and the groove will be easily played.

Remember, every time you find a bass line with tied notes, the process to learn it is always the same: simplify it, learn and master it, and finally, let the note ring until the next attack.
You will find yourself playing what looked complex at first sight easy to play.

Analysis of Example 10.5

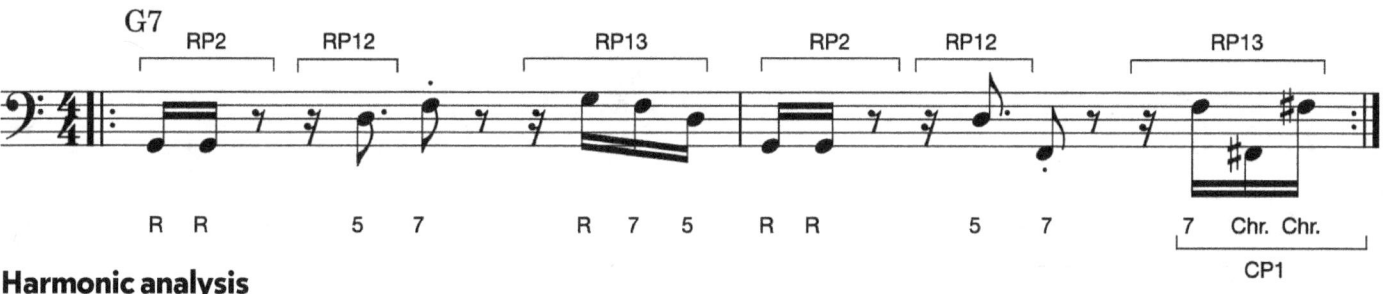

Harmonic analysis

We use the root, 5th, and 7th of the G7 chord (G, D, F) together with the chromatic passing note F♯ between the 7th (F) and the root (G), CP1: M2-B4.

Rhythmic analysis

RP2: M1-B1, M2-B1
RP12: M1-B2, M2-B2
RP13: M1-B4, M2-B4

PLAYING TECHNIQUE: DOUBLE STOPS

Double stops refer to the technique of playing two notes at the same time, it is a nice guitar like comping effect to add to our bass lines.
Many intervals can be played, but for our purposes, we will play the 3rd and 7th of the chord as it is a great sound to apply to funk bass lines.

Let's learn the two 3rd-7th , 7th-3rd intervals of C7.

▶ Example 10.6: C7 Double Stops

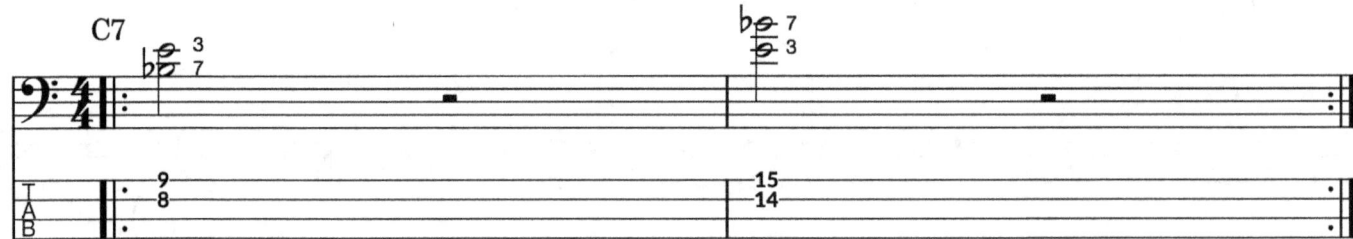

In the first measure, we play the 7th (B♭) and the 3rd (E) on top, while in the second measure, we play the 3rd (E) and the 7th (B♭) on top. They both use the same notes but in a different order.
Double stops are often played by sliding half a step into the final notes, like a guitar player typically does when comping.

Listen to the nice effect.

▶ Example 10.7: C7 Double Stops, Half Step Slide

Let's try this new technique.

10.8: C7 Groove with Double Stops

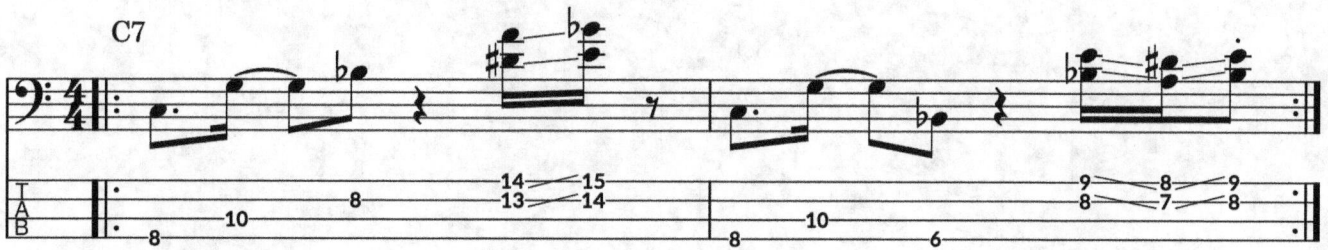

Analysis of Example 10.8

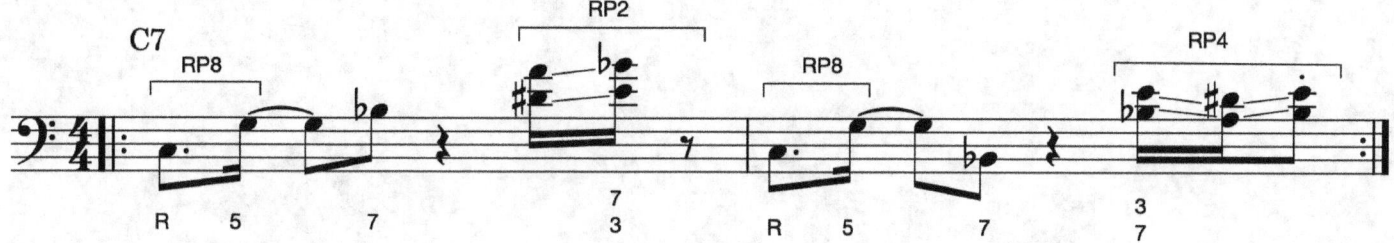

Harmonic analysis

The main notes of the groove are the root, 3rd, and 7th (C, G, B♭), while the double stops are the 3rd and 7th (E, B♭) of the C7 chord.

In the first measure, we make a half-step slide into the double stop notes. In the second measure, we do a double slide; first, a half step down, and then back again to the double stop notes (B♭, E).

Rhythmic analysis

RP2: M1-B4
RP4: M1-B2
RP8: M1-B1, M2-B1

SUMMARY

- **Chromatic pattern CP4 is added to your vocabulary. It connects the 2nd to the 3rd, and when applied in a bass line, we can now produce a more dense chromatic effect.**

- **Understand that any complex rhythm with tied notes can be simplified to its fundamental rhythmic patterns for ease of learning.**

- **The sound of the two intervals of a double stop, built with the 3rd and the 7th of the chord, can add a nice 'guitar slide' effect to bass lines.**

LESSON

OBJECTIVES

- **Chromatic Pattern 5**
- **Minor 7th chord**
- **The Dorian scale**

11

CHROMATIC PATTERN 5

Let's contiinue our exploration of chromatic notes with the last chromatic pattern on a dominant 7 chord, CP5, which connects the root to the 2nd of the 7th chord; it is not used often like other chromatic passing notes, but when it is used, it gives an interesting chromatic sound to the bass line.

See below the example with the #1 or ♭2 chromatic notes (diamond note head).

Example 11.1: Chromatic Pattern 5

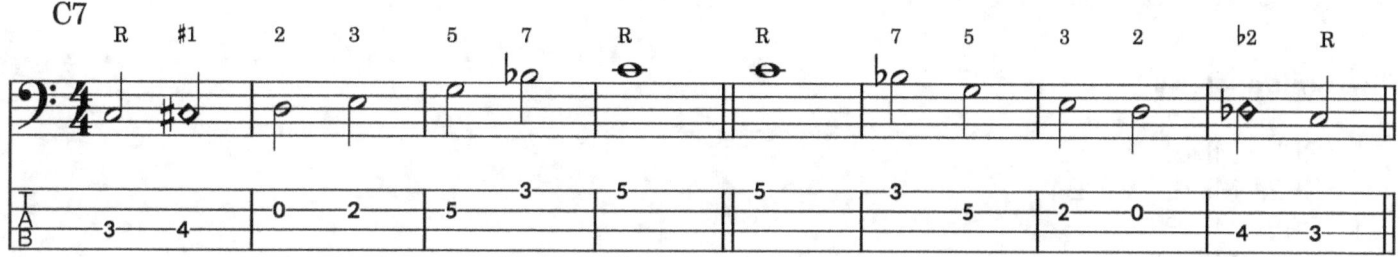

This chromatic pattern is primarily used with notes descending from the 2nd to the root.

As mentioned in previous lessons, the approach notes always tend to resolve to a chord tone, and in this case, to the root.

Let's apply this chromatic pattern in the next groove.

Example 11.2: Groove with CP5 in E7

Analysis of Example 11.2

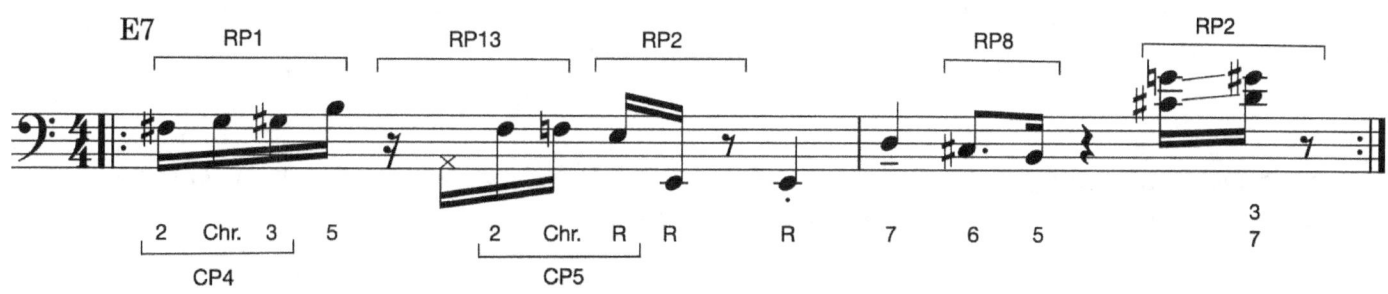

Harmonic analysis

It is certainly possible to create an exciting groove by starting on a chord tone other than the root, as seen in this example.

Here we use all of the chord tones of the E7 chord (E, B, G♯, D), plus the 2nd (F♯) and the 6th (C♯).

In the first beat of the first measure, we use a chromatic passing note, G, between the 2nd (F♯) and the 3rd (G♯), we use CP4: M1-B1.
In the second beat of the measure, we use the chromatic note F (natural) between the 2nd (F♯) and the Root (E) instead, this becomes CP5: M1-B3.
In the last beat of measure two, we use a chromatic slide to the double stop with the 7th (D) and the 3rd (G♯) on top.

Rhythmic analysis

RP1:   M1-B1
RP2:   M1-B3, M2-B4
RP8:   M2-B2
RP13: M1-B2

MINOR 7TH CHORD

In the previous lessons, we explored all the notes available over a 7th chord, and we learned the critical relationships between the chord tones and the bass line, the additional notes available, the five possible chromatic notes, and double stops.

Now that we have exhausted all the harmonic possibilities to create a bass line over a 7th chord, we can apply that knowledge to a new chord, the minor 7th chord.

The only difference between the 7th chord and the minor 7th lies in the third of the chord, which is minor instead of major.

▶ **Example 11.3: Gm7 Arpeggio**

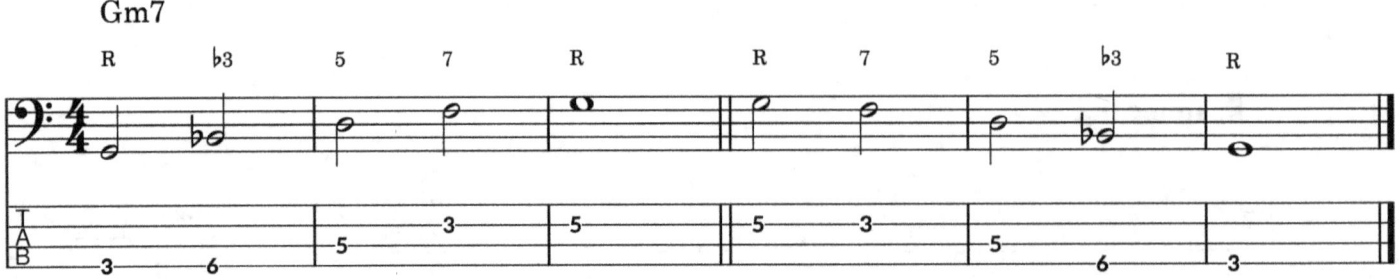

Formula: The fingering to play this arpeggio is **1-4–3-1-3** and can be used for all min7 arpeggios. Try practicing with different roots using the same formula.

Note: The G minor 7 chord can be notated as Gmin7, Gm7, or G-7. Any of the notations can be used, in our lessons, we will use Gm7.

 Example 11.4: Gm7 Groove

Let's play a groove build with the Gm7 arpeggio.

Analysis of Example 11.4

Harmonic analysis

In this groove we use the root, 3rd and 7th of Gm7 (G, B♭, F).

Rhythmic analysis

RP3: M1-B4
RP4: M2-B4
RP9: M1-B1/B2, M2-B1/B2

THE DORIAN SCALE

It is important to understand that the additional passing notes available for the Min7 chord are the same as in the 7th chord.

If we add the major 2nd, the perfect 4th, and the major 6th to the chord tones, we would then have the Dorian scale (another mode of the major scale).

▶ Example 11.5: G Dorian Scale

In the G Dorian scale, A is the 2nd, C is the 4th, and E is the 6th.

We use these notes in the same way as the 7th chord. They are additional passing notes that can be used with the chord tones to create more compelling bass lines.
We also use the chromatic patterns we have studied to connect chord tones to passing notes chromatically.
However, there is one exception, CP4, we cannot use it because there isn't a major 3rd to connect the minor 7th chord.

Let's play a groove in minor.

▶ Example 11.6: Gm7 Groove

Analysis of Example 11.6

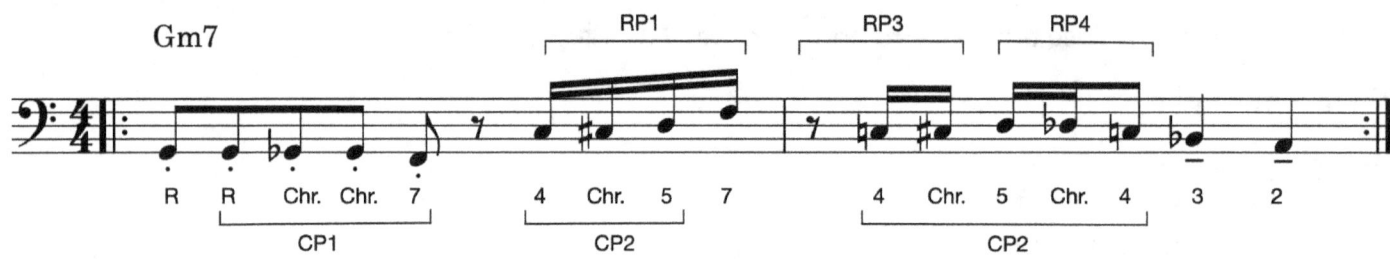

Harmonic analysis

We use all the chord tones of Gm7 (G, B♭, D, F) together with the 4th (C) and the 2nd (A).
In the second beat of the first measure, we have a chromatic passing note, G♭, between the root (G) and the 7th (F), CP1: M1-B2.
We use the chromatic note C♯ between the 4th (C) and the 5th (D) three times: CP2: M1-B4, M2-B1/B2.

Rhythmic analysis

RP1: M1-B4
RP3: M2-B1
RP4: M2-B2

▶ Example 11.7: Am7 Groove

Tip: Before practicing this example, play the Am7 arpeggio and the A Dorian scale. This will help you recognize all the available notes before attempting to play the groove.

Analysis of Example 11.7

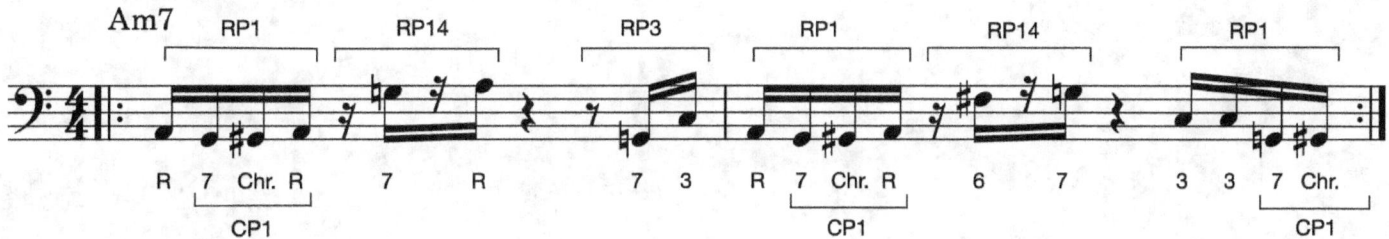

Harmonic analysis

We use the root, 3rd, and 7th of the Am7 chord (A, C, G) , the 6th (F♯), plus the chromatic note G♯ between the 7th (G) and the Root (A) three times: CP1: M1-B1, M2-B1/B4.

Rhythmic analysis

RP1:   M1-B1, M2-B1/B4
RP3:   M1-B4
RP14: M1-B2, M2-B2

In the last two grooves, we used all of the chord tones and extensions (2nd, 4th, and 6th) the same way we use them over a 7th chord.

You may have noticed the difference between the min7 and 7th chords, the Dorian and the Mixolydian scale is only one note, the 3rd (minor instead of major).

SUMMARY

- **Having learned CP5, we have now learned all of the available chromatic notes and now have all the tools to build bass lines over a 7th chord.**

- **We learned the min7th chord and played its arpeggio. We also highlighted the difference between the 7th chord and minor 7th chord: minor 3rd instead of a major one.**

- **The Dorian scale is the reference for the min7 chords. It contains the chord tones and the available extensions used to build bass lines.**

LESSON

Objectives

- **Chromatic Pattern 6**
- **Groove in a chord progression**
- **Chromatic notes that connect chords**

CHROMATIC PATTERN 6

We finally come to the last chromatic pattern, this new pattern applies to minor chords only because it connects the minor 3rd to the 4th.

There is a whole tone between the two notes, therefore we can use a chromatic note between them to add to our chromatic patterns vocabulary.

See in the example below the chromatic note with the diamond shape.

▶ Example 12.1: Chromatic Pattern 6

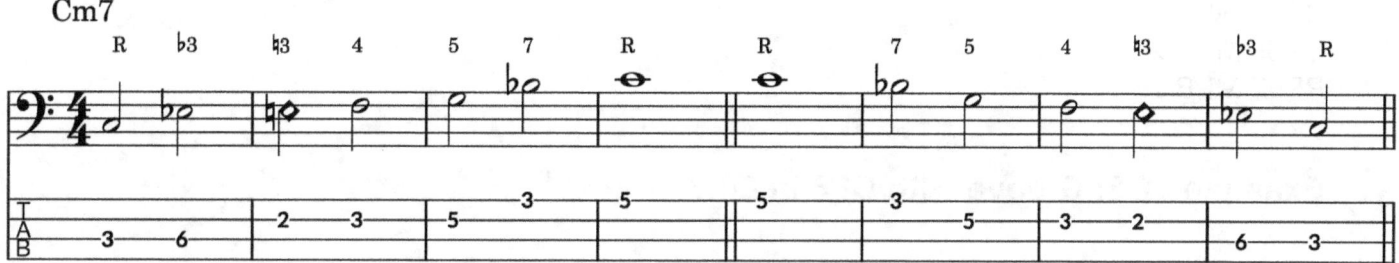

This pattern can be used freely since the 4th in minor chords is not as dissonant sound as it is in 7th chords.

Notice the different fingering used here compared to what we normally use for the min7 arpeggio. We shift the first finger to play the chromatic note. However, as we will see in the grooves, there are other and simpler ways to play it.

Let's apply this chromatic pattern in the next groove.

▶ Example 12.2: Groove with CP6 in Cm7

Analysis of Example 12.2

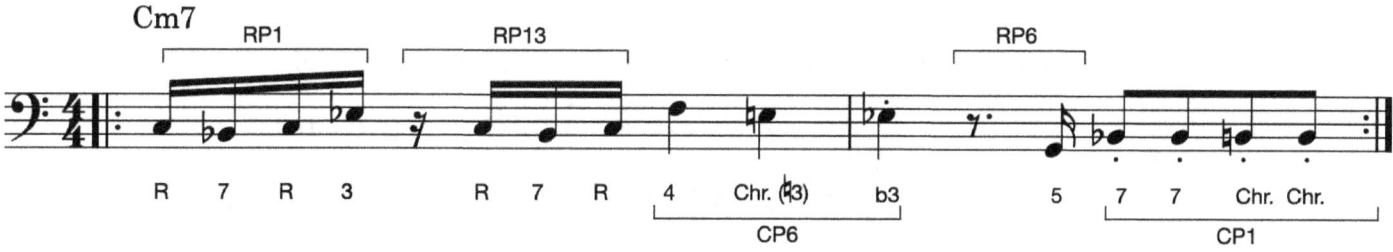

Harmonic Analysis

We play all the chord tones of the Cm7 chord (C, E♭, G, B♭) plus the 4th (F), and use two chromatic notes.

One in the fourth beat of the first measure, the chromatic passing note E, between the 4th (F) and the minor 3rd (E♭), we use the new CP6: M1-B4.
In the last beat of measure two, we use B natural as a chromatic note from the 7th (B♭) to the Root, CP1: M2-B4.

Rhythmic Analysis

RP1:   M1-B1
RP6:   M2-B2
RP13: M1-B2

 ### Example 12.3: Groove with CP6 in Em7

In this example, CP6 is used together with CP1 and CP2 on a Em7 chord.

Analysis of Example 12.3

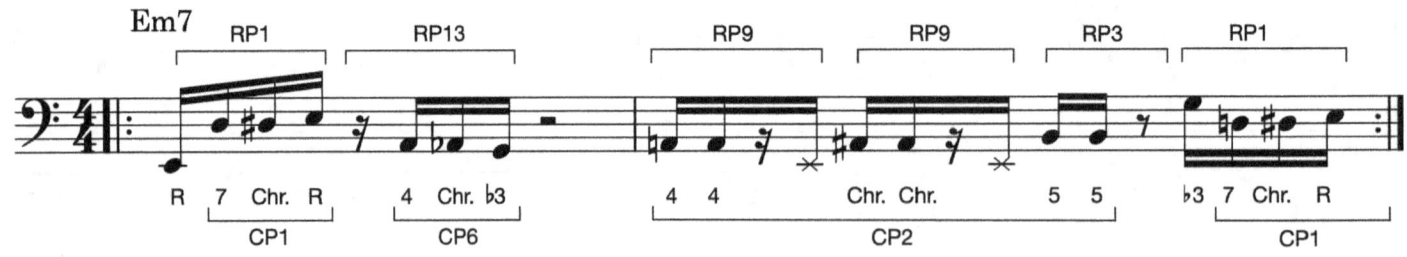

Harmonic Analysis

The groove contains all the notes of the Em7 chord (E, G, B, D) and the 4th (A).

We use three chromatic passing notes; the Ab connecting the 4th (A) to the minor 3rd (G) in measure one, beat 2 is CP6: M1-B2.
In measure two, A♯ connects the 4th (A) to the 5th (B), CP2: M2-B2, and in the first beat of measure one and the last beat of measure two, the D♯ connects the 7th to the root, CP1: M2-B4.

Rhythmic Analysis

RP1:   M1-B1, M2-B4
RP2:   M2-B3
RP9:   M2-B1/B2
RP13: M1-B2

GROOVE ON A CHORD PROGRESSION

In contemporary funk music, it is rare to play a tune that contains only one chord, instead, it would likely be a progression made of different chords like the 7th, min7, or another kind.

We will play a few grooves to demonstrate two fundamental principles, repetition and extension.

Example 12.4: Repeated Groove over Dm7 and G7 Progression

This line uses the fundamental principle of creating a bass line over a progression, repeating the same groove starting from the Root of another chord.

When playing the same pattern over a different chord, it is critical to ensure the use of the correct chord tones.

Analysis of Example 12.4

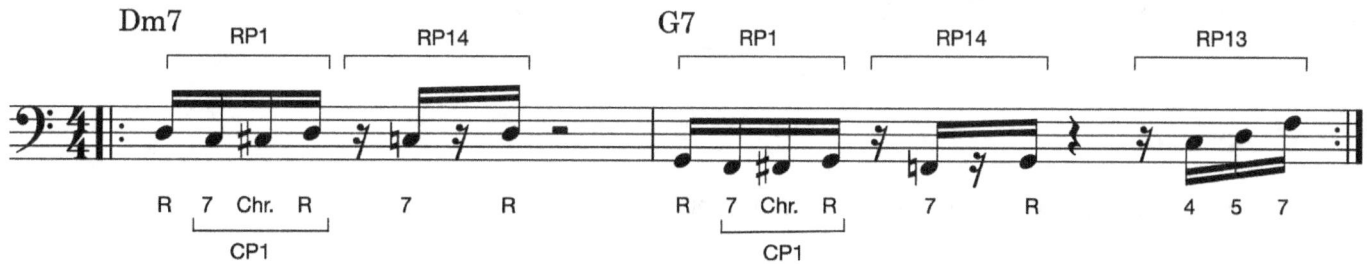

Harmonic Analysis

The groove contains the root and 7th of the Dm7 (D, C), and the root, 5th, and 7th of G7 (G, D, F) plus the 4th (C) as a passing note.

We use the chromatic passing notes between the Root and the 7th in both chords, C♯ on Dm7 and F♯ on G7; CP1: M1-B1/M2-B1.

Rhythmic Analysis

RP1: M1-B1, M2-B1
RP13: M2-B4
RP14: M1-B2, M2-B2

▶ Example 12.5: Extended Groove Over Dm7 and G7 Progression

In the next groove, we change the basic principle of repetition. Here we extend the groove by one measure by changing the rhythmic figure in the second measure to give it a more sophisticated sound.

Analysis of Example 12.5

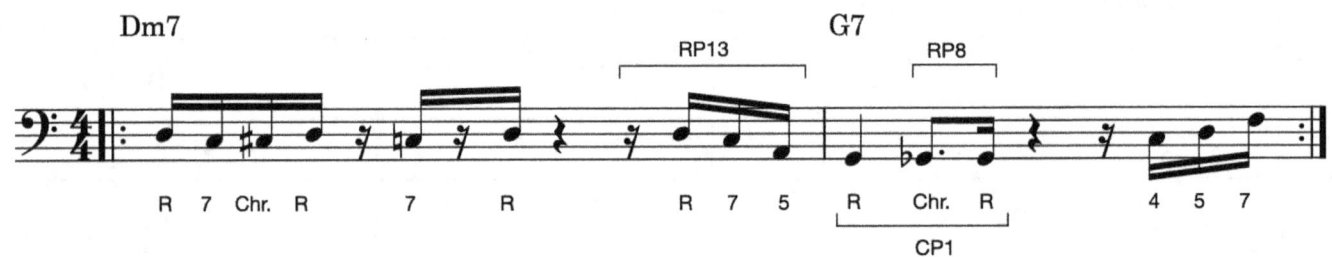

Harmonic Analysis

In this variation, we use root, 5th, and 7th over Dm7 and introduce the chromatic passing note G♭ between the root and the 7th of G7: CP1: M2-B2.

Rhythmic Analysis

Changes in the rhythm from the previous example.

RP8: M2-B1
RP13: M1-B4

If you review the previous lessons, you will notice that most of the bass lines use this concept of extending the groove over two measures, especially when using a single chord.

Keep these two principles in mind when creating your own bass lines, especially the extension; it will help you to avoid being too repetitive.

CHROMATIC NOTES CONNECTING CHORDS

So far, we have analyzed chromatic passing notes used within the same chord. As we progress through the lessons, the chord progressions we will encounter will use chromatic notes that do not belong to any pattern because they connect different chords and not chord tones.

See the following example.

▶ Example 12.6: Chromatic Notes Between Dm7 and G7 Progression

Analysis of Example 12.6

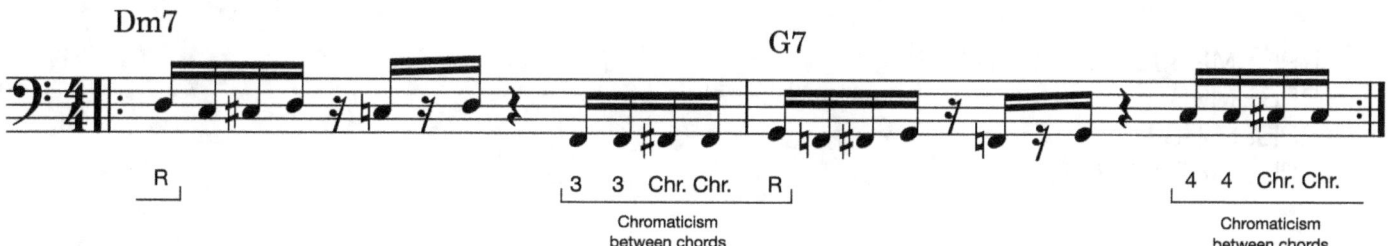

Harmonic Analysis

At the end of measure one, we use F♯ to connect the 3rd (F) of Dm7 to the root of G7 (G), then at the end of measure two, we use C♯ to connect the 4th (C) of G7 to the root of Dm7 (D).

These notes don't belong to any chromatic pattern because they connect chord tones or passing notes to a different chord.

▶ Example 12.7: Chromatic Notes Between Em7 and A7 Progression

Below is another example of this chromatic device used in a different key:

Analysis of Example 12.7

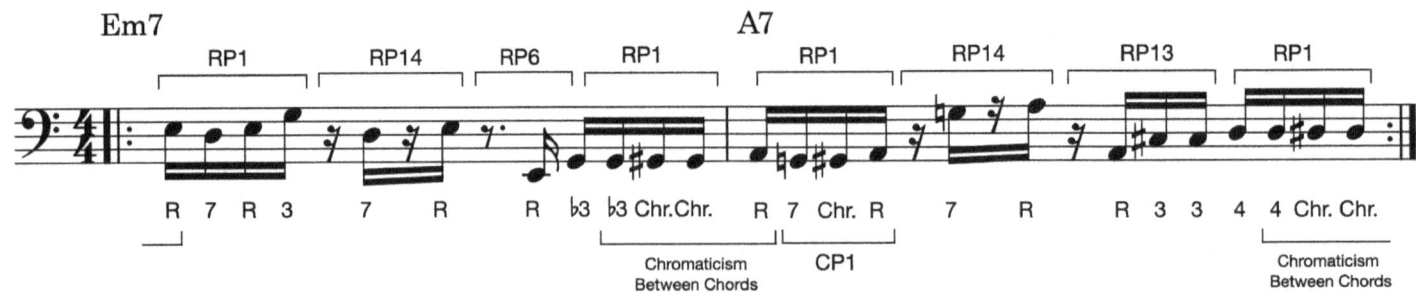

Harmonic analysis

In the first measure, the root, 3rd, 7th of Em7 (E, G, D) are used together with a chromatic note (G♯) connecting the minor 3rd (G) to the root of the next measure (A).

In the second measure, we use the root, 3rd, and 7th of A7 (A, C♯, G), the 4th (D), and two chromatic notes. G♯, which connects the 7th (G) and the root (A), making it CP1: M2-B1, and the second chromatic note is D♯ connects the 4th (D) to the root of the Em7 chord.

Rhythmic analysis

RP1:   M1-B1/B4. M2-B1/B4
RP6:   M1-B3
RP13: M2-B3
RP14: M1-B2, M2-B2

Summary

- **CP6 is a chromatic passing note used only in minor chords – it connects the minor 3rd to the 4th.**

- **Two main principles in creating bass lines on multiple chords are repeating the same pattern in another chord and extending the bass line over the next measure by changing its rhythm.**

- **Chromatic notes are not only limited within a chord. They can occur between chords, connecting a chord tone or a passing note to the next root.**

LESSON

PLAYING TECHNIQUE: DOUBLE STOPS ON MINOR 7 CHORDS

In Lesson 10, we learned how to create double stops over a 7th chord using the 3rd and the 7th.

The same principle applies over a minor 7 (min7) chord, using the same chord tones, 3rd, and 7th, to create the double stops.

Below are the two possible intervals with the 3rd and 7th of the min7 chord.

▶ Example 13.1: Gm7 Double Stops

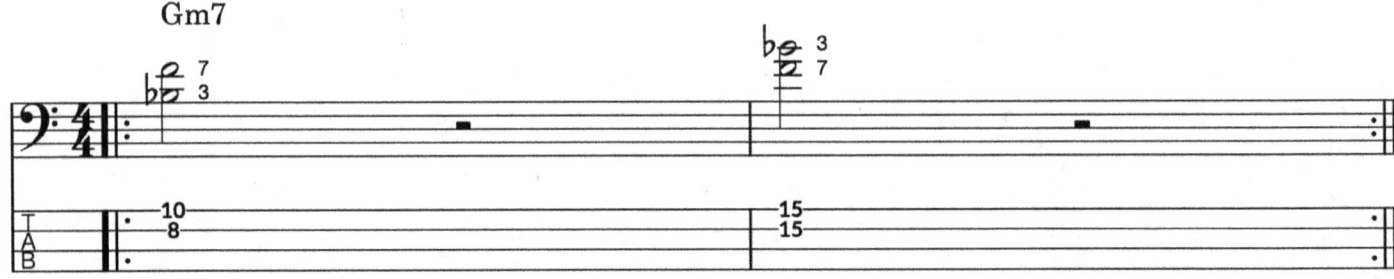

In the first measure, we play the 3rd (B♭) and the minor 7th (F) on top, while in the second measure, we play the 7th (F) and the minor 3rd (B♭) on top.

Like the double stops on the 7th chord, the two notes can be played by sliding them a half step into the final notes.

▶ Example 13.2: Gm7 Double stops half step slide

Let's apply the second shape over a Gm7 chord.

▶ Example 13.3: Gm7 Groove with Double Stops

Analysis of Example 13.3

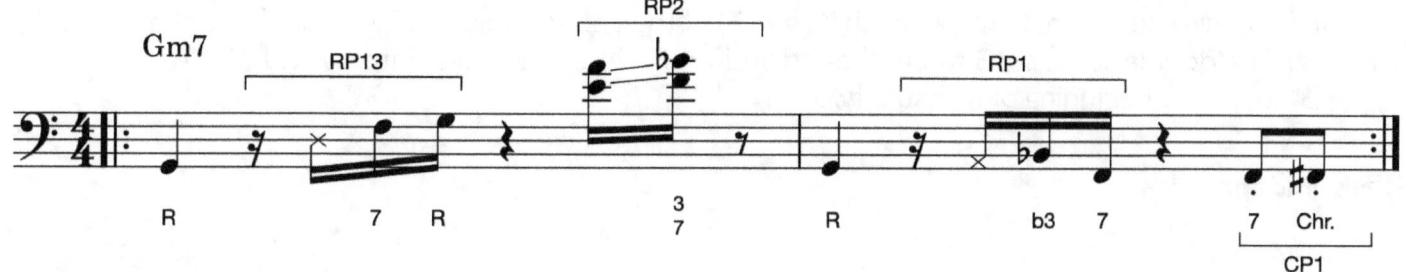

Harmonic analysis

The main notes of the groove are the root, 3rd, and 7th (G, B♭, and F), while the double stops are the 3rd and 7th (F, B♭) of the Gm7 chord.

In the first measure, we do a half-step slide into the double stop notes.

The F♯ at the end of the second measure is a chromatic passing note connecting the 7th (F) to the root (G), CP1: M2-B4.

Rhythmic analysis

RP2: M1-B4
RP13: M1-B2, M2-B2

DOUBLE STOPS OVER A CHORD PROGRESSION

Now that we've learned about double stops on 7th and min7 chords, we can mix both shapes over a common chord progression to create a compelling funk sound on the bass.

Example 13.4: Double Stops Over Gm7 and C7

Analysis of Example 13.4

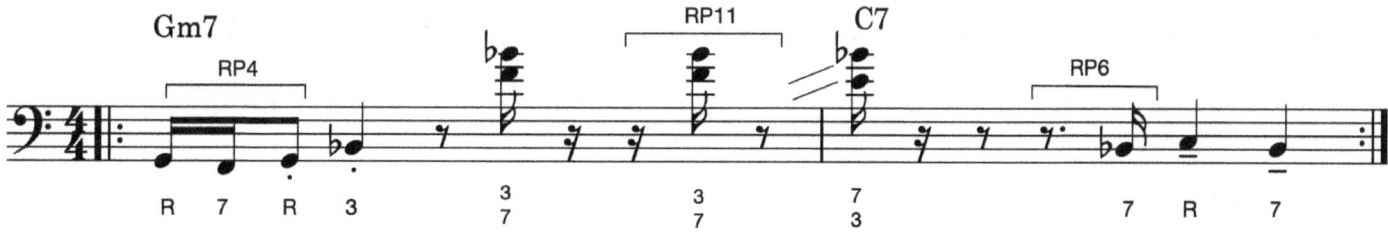

Harmonic analysis

In Gm7, we use the root, 3rd, and 7th (G, B♭, F) of the chord, while in C7, we use the root and 7th (C, B♭). The double stops on Gm7 are the 3rd and 7th (F, B♭), and we slide into C7 with the 7th and 3rd (B♭, E) at the beginning of measure two.

Rhythmic analysis

RP4: M1–B1
RP6: M2–B3
RP11: M1–B4

The sixteenth notes on M1-B3 and M2-B1 are simple and short upbeat and downbeat, therefore, not marked as RP.

In the following example, the chord progression has two 7th chords.

Example 13.5: Double Stops Over E7 and A7

Analysis of Example 13.5

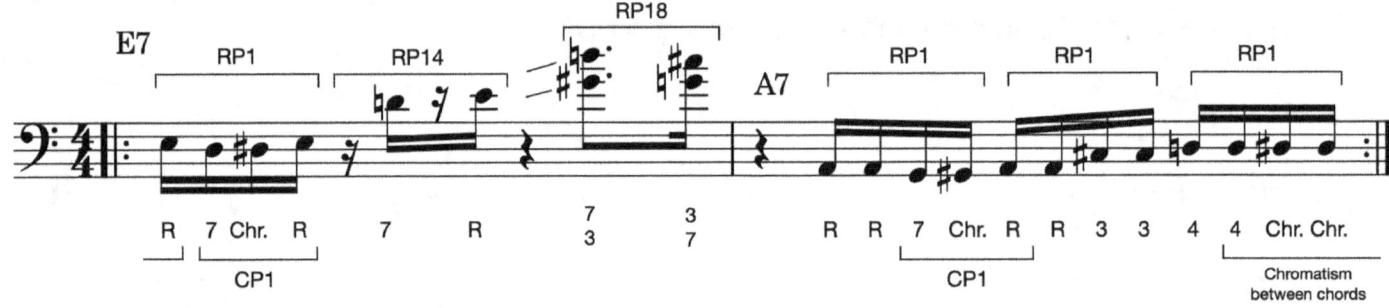

Harmonic analysis

In E7, we use the root and 7th (E, D) of the chord plus the D♯ between the 7th (D) and the root (E), CP1: M1–B1.

In A7, we use the root, 3rd, and 7th (A, C♯, G), plus the 4th (D), together with the D♯ connecting to the E7 chord.
The G♯ in measure two is the chromatic passing note between the 7th (G) and the root of A7; thus, CP1: M2–B2.

The double stops on E7 are the 3rd and 7th (G♯, D), and on the last sixteenth note of measure one, is an anticipation of the A7 notes (G, C♯).

Rhythmic analysis

RP1:   M1–B1, M2–B2/B3/B4
RP18: M1–B4
RP14: M1–B2

THE MINOR PENTATONIC SCALE

A pentatonic scale is a scale with five notes per octave. There are different types of pentatonic scales, but for this course we will focus mainly on the Minor Pentatonic.

The scale is comprised of a minor 7 arpeggio plus the 4th.
This is the Minor Pentatonic in A.

▶ **Example 13.6: Minor Pentatonic in A**

To get the most out of the Pentatonic scale, it is necessary to extend the scale on the G string by adding the C and D one octave higher. In this way, we use all of the notes available in a single hand position.

▶ **Example 13.7: Minor Pentatonic in A, Extended**

Now that you can play the full extension of the scales, we will learn one of the most used melodic patterns that work well in grooves and fills.

▶ **Example 13.8: Minor Pentatonic Pattern in A**

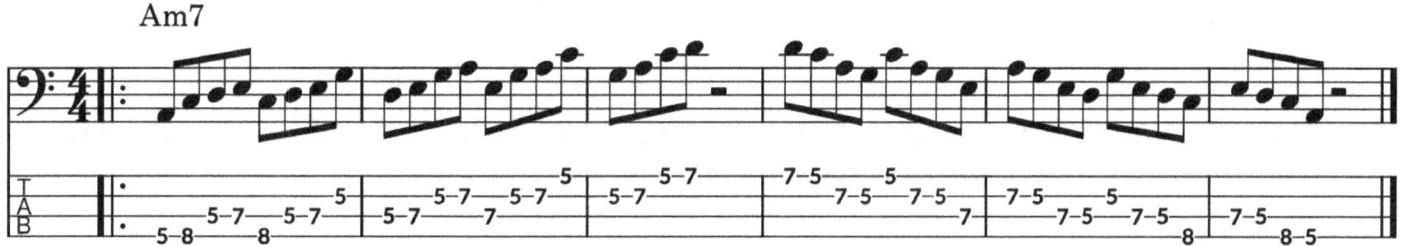

The pattern consists of playing the notes of the pentatonic scales in groups of four notes.

Tip: Pay close attention to the fingering used to play this pattern and practice it slowly!

Let's apply this pattern to a groove.

▶ Example 13.9: Groove in Am7 with Minor Pentatonic Patterns

Analysis of Example 13.9

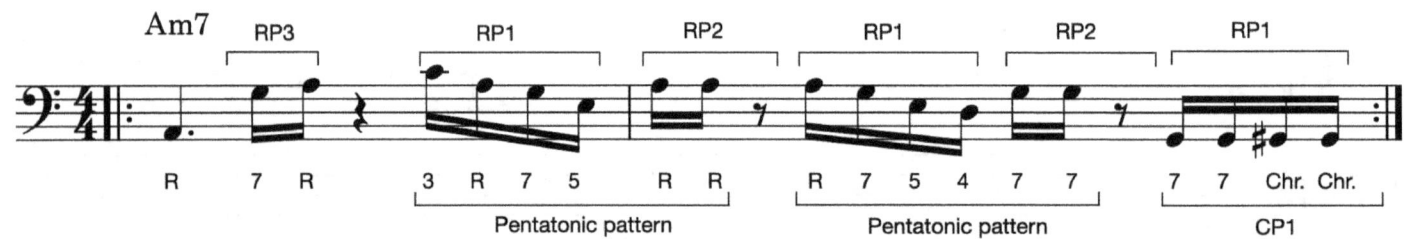

Harmonic analysis

In this groove, we use all of the notes of the A Minor Pentatonic scale (that includes all of the notes of the Am7 chord (A, C, E, G) plus the 4th (D).
We use the G# between the root (A) and the 7th (G): CP1: M2-B4.

Rhythmic analysis

RP1: M1-B1, M2-B2/B4
RP2: M2-B1/B3
RP3: M1-B2

We will encounter this pattern again when we learn about fills.

SUMMARY

- **CP6 is a chromatic passing note used only in minor chords – it connects the minor 3rd to the 4th.**

- **Two main principles in creating bass lines on multiple chords are repeating the same pattern in another chord and extending the bass line over the next measure by changing its rhythm.**

- **Chromatic notes are not only limited within a chord. They can occur between chords, connecting a chord tone or a passing note to the next root.**

LESSON

OBJECTIVES

- **The Blues Scale**
- **The Blues Scale over the 7th chord.**
- **Fills**

THE BLUES SCALE

The Blues scale and its unique sound is used in many genres, including Blues, Rock, Jazz, Country, and Funk.

The scale is essentially a Minor Pentatonic scale with a chromatic note between the 4th and the 5th, often called the "blue note", producing its unmistakably bluesy sound.

The scale is used in solos and for creating distinct melodies and grooves. We will be using it mainly for grooves and fills.

Below is the blues scale in A.

▶ Example 14.1: A Blues Scale

The D♯ (E♭) is the ♯4 (or ♭5) of the scale and is referred to as the blue note.

This note is the same note used in CP2 (♯4), however CP2 does not sound very bluesy because the chromatic note is used as a passing note, connecting the 4th to the 5th.
In the Blues scale, the blue note is often used alone and does not connect anything.

Let's apply the Blues scale to a groove.

▶ Example 14.2: Am7 Groove with the Blues Scale

Analysis of Example 14.2

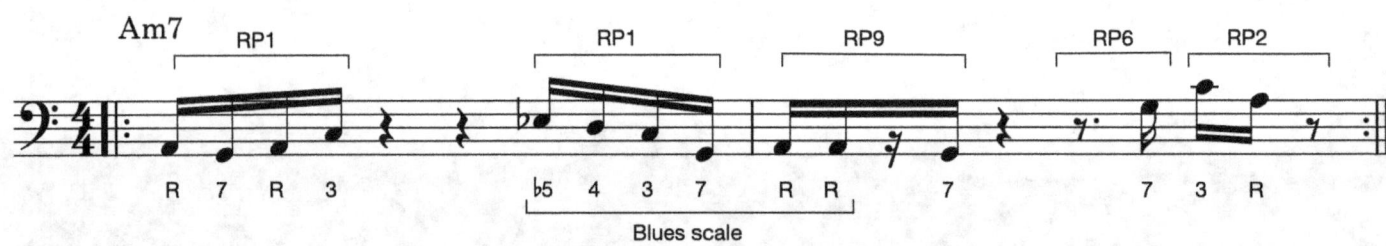

Harmonic analysis

As you can see, the A Blues scale contains all of the chord tones in Am7 (A, C, E, G), and here they are used to create the groove as in the previous lessons.
Additionally, we have the blue note (E♭) and the 4th (D).

We can see that there is no chromatic pattern (CP2), the E♭ does not connect the 5th to the 4th because the 5th is missing; it is used to give the groove a bluesy sound.

Rhythmic analysis

RP1:   M1-B2/B4
RP2:   M2-B4
RP6:   M2-B3
RP9:   M2-B1

We change keys now and play a grove in E, but before we do, let's learn a good fingering to play the E Blues scale.

▶ Example 14.3: E Blues scale

There are several fingerings possible for each scale, but this is a good one to play grooves in E. It is undoubtedly an excellent idea to explore other fingerings because it will expand your knowledge of the fingerboard.

▶ Example 14.4: Em7 Groove with the Blues Scale

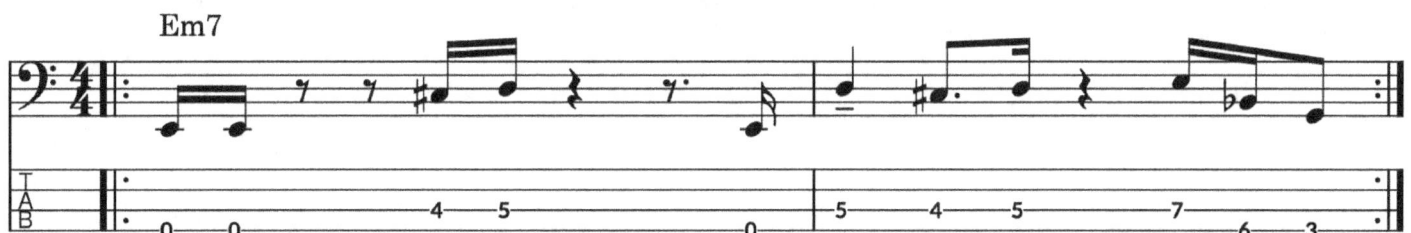

Analysis of Example 14.4

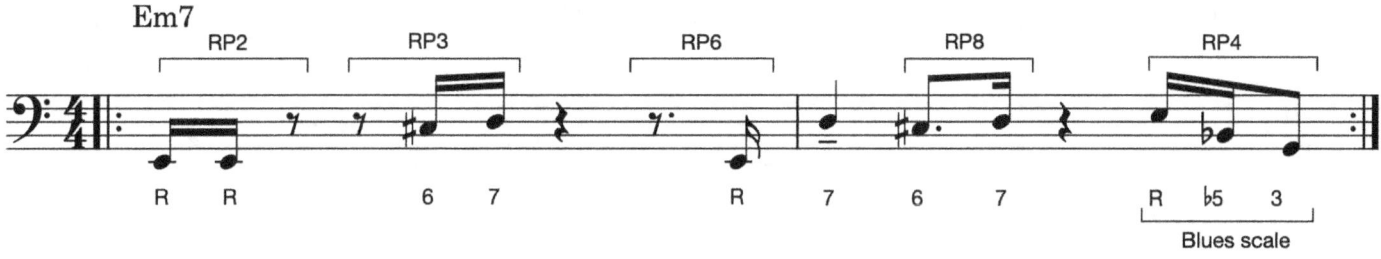

Harmonic analysis

This line is interesting harmonically because the Blues scale is used only in the last beat.

We use the Root and 7th (E, D) with the addition of the 6th (C♯), and only in the fourth beat of the second measure we use the blue note (B♭) of the E Blues scale together with the root (E) and the 3rd (G).

This is a typical example of how the Blues scale can be utilized in a groove as it can be mixed with other scales, like, in this case, a Dorian one.

Rhythmic analysis

RP2: M1–B1
RP3: M1–B2
RP4: M2–B4
RP6: M1–B4
RP8: M2–B2

THE BLUES SCALE OVER THE 7TH CHORD

In previous chapters, we used the Blues and the Pentatonic scales over a min7 chord, assuming that the minor 3rd of the scales are used over minor chords only. In reality, those scales can and are widely used on 7th chords.

In a Blues song, guitarists extensively use Blues and Pentatonic scales to solo, and bass players use them in the same manner to give a bluesy sound to their bass lines. We will do the same but in a Funk context.

Over a min7 chord, we had the choice to add a blue note to give a Bluesy sound to the bass line. Over a 7th chord, however, we have two options.

The blue note (♭5) and the minor 3rd of the Blues or Pentatonic scale, can be used alone or at the same time to give the desired sound.

Let's play a few examples.

▶ Example 14.5: A7 Groove with the Blues Scale

Analysis of Example 14.5

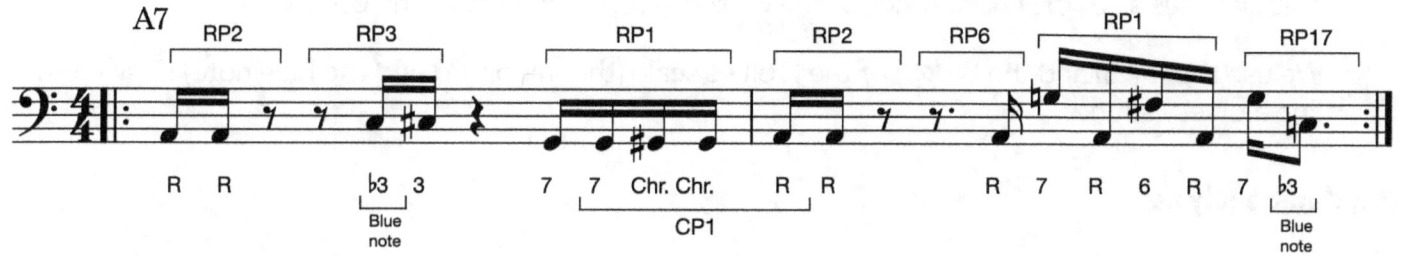

Harmonic analysis

This line uses the Root, 3rd, and 7th chord (A, C♯, G) plus the 6th (F♯).
We use the G♯ as a connecting note between the 7th (G) and the root (A), thus we use CP1: M1/B4.

The C natural gives the bluesy sound to this line (from the A Blues or Pentatonic scale).
It is important to note how the C natural is used. In the first measure, it is used as an approach note to the major 3rd of the chord in beat 2, and in the last beat of measure two, it is used alone.

Using the minor 3rd (♭3) as a passing note to the major 3rd or alone, are excellent ways to add a bluesy sound to your groove.

Rhythmic analysis

RP1: M1–B4, M2–B3   RP6: M2–B2
RP2: M1–B1, M2–B1   RP17: M2–B4
RP3: M1–B2

 ## Example 14.6: E7 Groove with the Blues Scale

Below is another example of mixing the sounds of the Mixolydian and Blues scales.

Analysis of Example 14.6

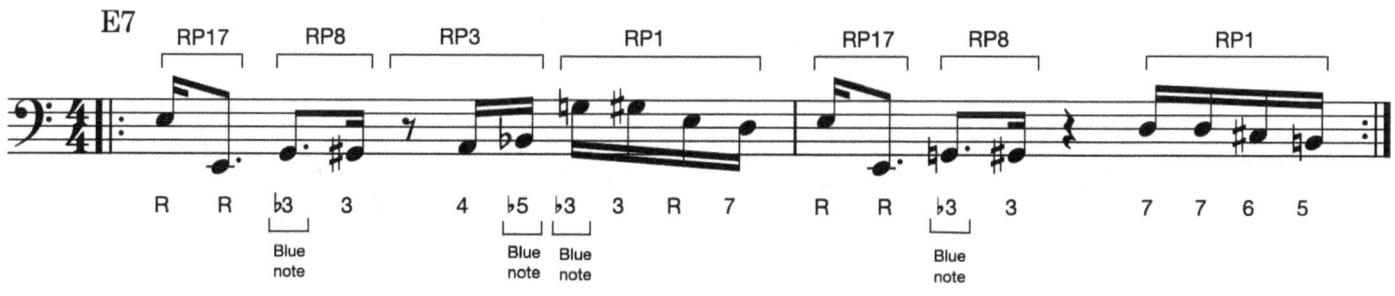

Harmonic analysis

This line uses all of the chord tones of the E7 chord (E, G♯, B, D) plus the 6th (C♯).

We use the G (♭3) and the B♭ (♭5) of the E blues scale (the minor 3rd and the blue note) to give the line a bluesy sound.

Rhythmic analysis

RP1:   M1-B4, M2-B4
RP3:   M1-B3
RP8:   M1-B2, M2-B2
RP17: M1-B1, M2-B1

FILLS

A fill is a short musical idea, usually one or two measures, that captures attention and usually signals the end of a section of a tune or a repeated cycle of measures.

The idea is typically more scalar, meaning we deviate from the groove feel and create another musical idea with a distinct character, then reconnect it to the initial feel.

The melodic sources to create fills include scales, chromatic notes, pentatonic, and blues scales, arpeggios - all the elements we have already learned!

▶ Example 14.7: A7 Groove with a Fill

Analysis of Example 14.7

Fill analysis

The fill in measure two is a mixture of three elements: the A Blues scale (A, C, D, E♭, E, G), the added major 3rd of the A7 (C♯) in the Blue scale and the chromatic note G♯, which is used to connect the 7th of the chord (G) back to the root (A), CP1.

We apply the same principles to create a variety of bass lines, incorporating them into a single phrase.

Let's play another fill, this time build with the Mixolydian scale.

▶ Example 14.8: A7 Groove with a Fill

Analysis of Example 14.8

Fill analysis

The fill is based only on the A Mixolydian scale, except for the last chromatic note, G♯, which is CP1.

SUMMARY

- **With the Blues scale, we expanded the sound of the Pentatonic scale by adding the blue note, and we are now able to add a bluesy feeling to our bass lines.**

- **The Blues and the Pentatonic scales can be used on the 7th chord. The clash between the major third of the chord and the minor third of the scale adds to the bluesy feel.**

- **Fills are short melodic ideas that add excitement at the end of a musical section and are built with the same melodic sources used with grooves.**

LESSON

OBJECTIVES

- **Fills, continued**
- **Other types of chords**
- **The creative process**

15

FILLS, CONTINUED

In the previous lesson, we learned that a bass fill can be created using a variety of melodic sources from our vocabulary. In the following example, we combine the Minor Pentatonic scale with the notes played in an arpeggio.

▶ Example 15.1: A7 Groove with a Fill

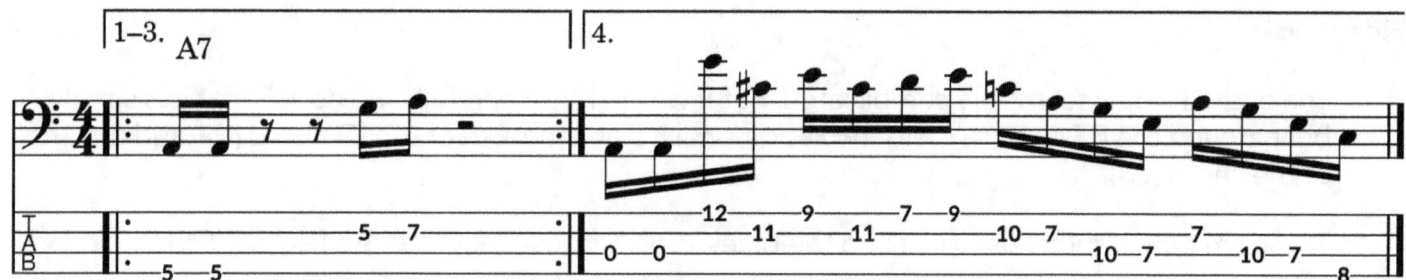

Analysis of Example 15.1

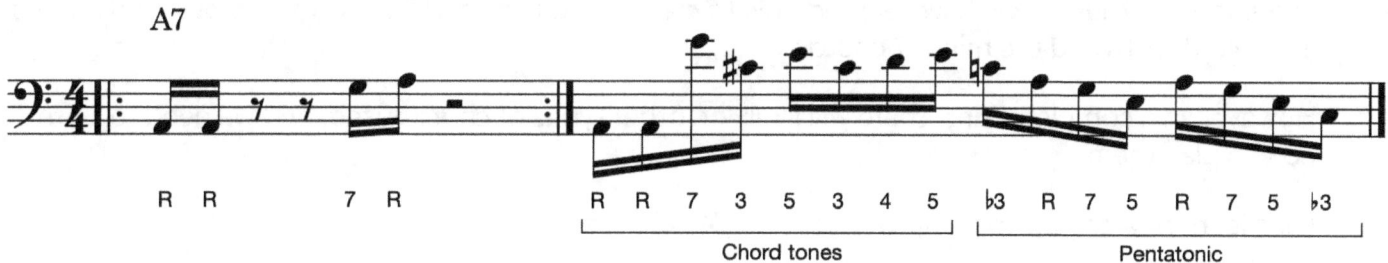

Fill analysis

In the first beat of the measure, we use only the chord tones of A7 (A, C♯, G) and the 4th. From the second beat to the end of the measure, we use the A minor Pentatonic scale. In the last two beats, we group the notes into four.

Can you hear the bluesy sound that is created with the minor pentatonic scale over the 7th chord?

▶ Example 15.2: E7 Groove with a Fill

Fills can span more than one measure, as in the example below.

Analysis of Example 15.2

Blues scale plus 3 and 6

Fill analysis

The entire fill may seem very complicated, but if we analyze it carefully, we notice that it is simply built around the E Blues scale with two additional notes - the 6th of the E7 chord (C♯) and the 3rd of the chord (G♯).

These are typical intervals to mix into the Blues scale because they create a less predictable sound.

OTHER TYPES OF CHORDS

In our lessons thus far, we have learned how to create bass lines and fills over the most used chords in Funk: the 7th and the minor 7 chords.

However, in a complete tune, there will likely be other types of chords used, and we need to learn how to play them.

Let's learn how to play the Major7 and Minor7♭5 chords.

▶ Example 15.3: CMaj7 Arpeggio

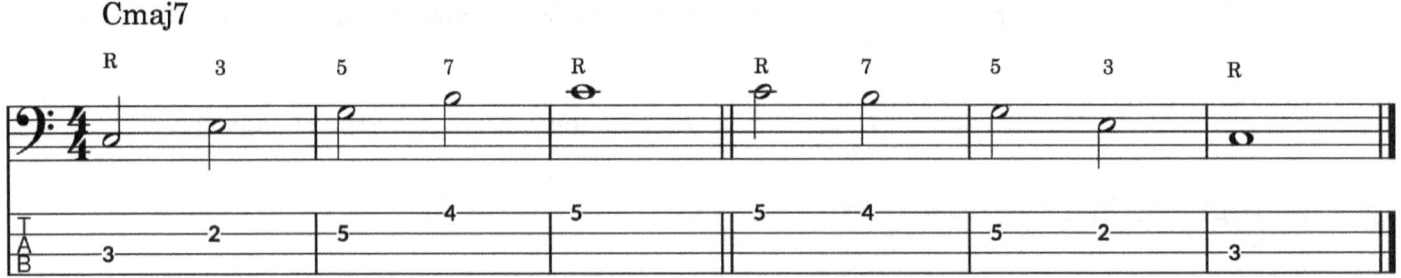

The Major 7 chord (Maj7) contains a B as the seventh of the chord. We will avoid using it in our bass lines as it doesn't create the funky sound we're aiming for.

To build a bass line, we should use the 6th, and add the same passing notes between the 3rd and the 5th and from the 5th to the 6th, as we did with previous chord types

See the next example.

▶ Example 15.4: CMaj7 Groove

Analysis of Example 15.4

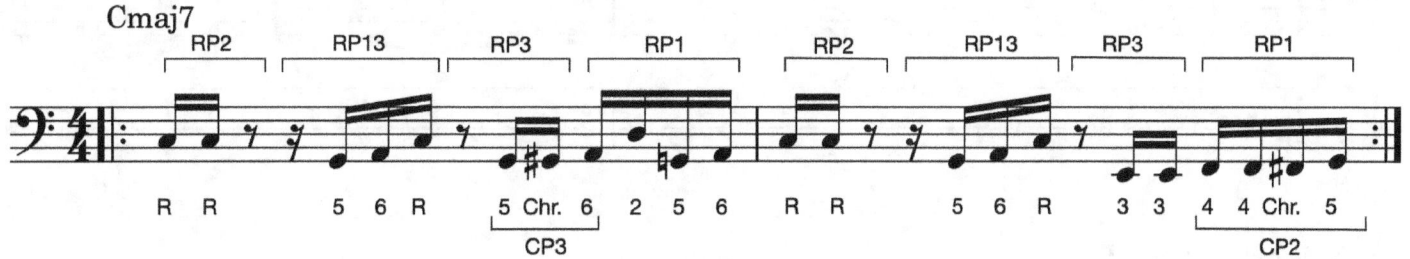

Harmonic analysis

This line uses the root, 3rd, and 7th (C, E, G), plus the 2nd (D) and 6th (A).

The F♯ connects the 4th (F) and the 5th (G): CP2: M2-B4, and the G♯ connects the 5th (G) and the 6th (A), we use CP3: M1-B3.
We use the same chromatic patterns as in the previous chords but intentionally avoid using the major 7th.

Rhythmic analysis

RP1: M1-B4, M2-B4
RP2: M1-B1, M2-B1
RP3: M1-B3, M2-B3
RP13: M1-B2, M2-B2

▶ Example 15.5: Cm7♭5 Arpeggio

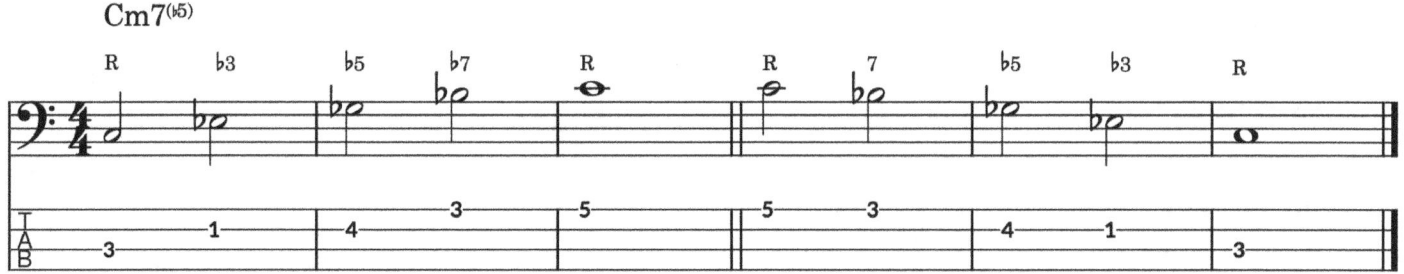

The difference between the min7 chord and the min7 chord lies in the use of the ♭5 (G♭) rather than the 5th (G). Although at times it is found in chord progressions, the sound of the chord is quite dark and not suited for Funk music.

Several scales can be used over this chord, but in practice, an interval-based approach to create a bass line over it is preferred.

We will use the chord tones of the arpeggio and will add the 4th (F) with CP1 and CP6.

Let's hear a line over this chord.

▶ Example 15.6: Cm7♭5 Groove

Analysis of Example 15.6

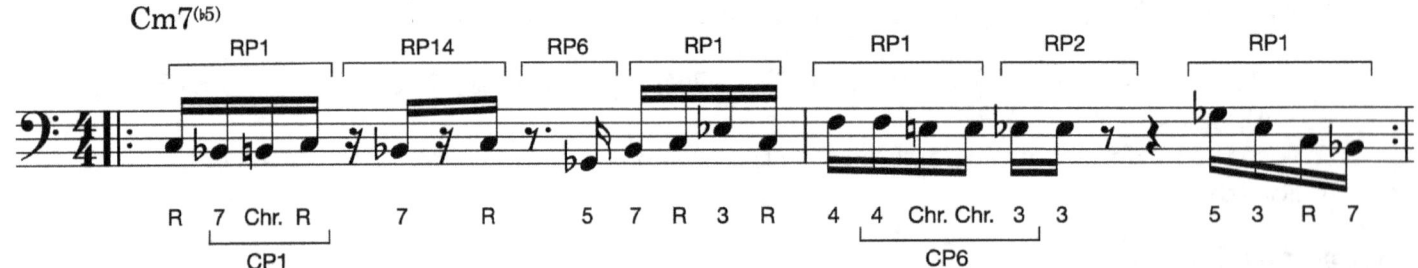

Harmonic analysis

This line uses all of the notes in the arpeggio (C, E♭, G♭, B♭) and the 4th (F).

The E connects the 4th (F), and the 3rd (E♭): CP6: M2-B1 and the B connects the 7th (B♭) and the root (C): CP1: M1-B1.

Notice in this groove that we use all the notes available over a Cm7♭5 chord. In practice, you can just use a few of them, for example, only the root and 7th.

Rhythmic analysis

RP1: M1-B1/B4, M2-B1/B4
RP2: M2-B2
RP6: M1/B3
RP14: M1-B2

Let's learn how to create a line over a jazz-type progression that uses these types of chords.

▶ Example 15.7: Dm7♭5 - G7♭9 - Cm7 Groove

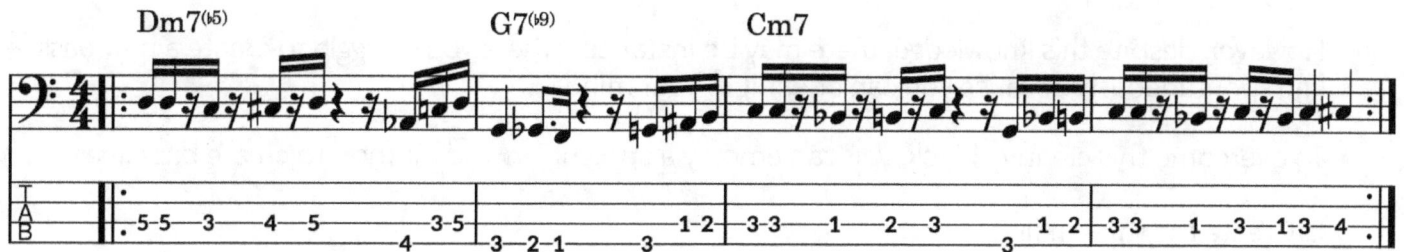

Analysis of Example 15.7

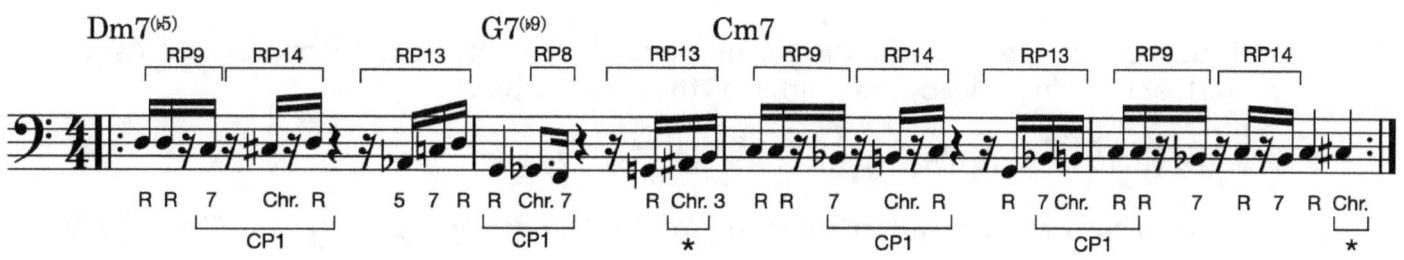

★ Chromatism connecting chords

Harmonic analysis

In the Dm7(♭5) chord, we use the root, ♭5, and 7th (D, C, A♭) plus the C♯ to connect the 7th (C) and the root (D), CP1: M1-B2.

In the G7(♭9) chord, we use the root, 3rd, and 7th (G, B, F) plus the chromatic notes G♭ to connect the root (G) to the 7th (F), CP1: M2-B2.

The A♯ together with the 3rd (B) to connect to the root of the next chord, Cm7.

The notes in the Cm7 are the root, 5th, and 7th (C, G, B♭), the B connects the root (C) and the 7th (B♭), CP1: M1-B2.

We also use a C♯ in the last measure to connect the root of the Cm7 chord to the root of the next chord, Dm7♭5.

Rhythmic analysis

RP8:   M2-B2
RP9:   M1-B1, M2-B4, M3-B1, M4-B1
RP13: M1-B4, M2-B4, M3-B4
RP14: M1-B2, M3-B2, M4-B2

THE CREATIVE PROCESS

By now, you should have acquired a comprehensive understanding of rhythmic patterns, the diverse sounds of chord tones, chromatic patterns, Blues, and Pentatonic scales. These fundamental elements equip you with the tools to spontaneously create Funk bass lines.

You now possess the tools to analyze bass lines and comprehend their rhythmic, harmonic, and chromatic features. This analytical process will not only reinforce your learning but also expand your musical vocabulary, enhancing your ability to craft original bass lines.

However, despite this knowledge, there may be instances where you struggle to create a new bass line spontaneously because you can't hear it in your mind.

To overcome this creative block, you can employ a straightforward method to create bass lines.

1. Create the rhythm first.

    Create two bars using the rhythmic patterns you already know. Make the second measure slightly different from the first.

2. Determine the chord/s

    Specify one or two chords for the two measures if this information is not provided. As you start, opt for simplicity by using either a 7th or min7 chord.

3. Add the chord tones to the rhythm

    Start to build your line with chord tones, root and the 7th first, and later, the 5th or the 3rd.

4. Add passing tones

    You can now add one or more passing tones to the bass line, or change chord tones in passing tones.

5. Add chromaticism to the line

    Finally you can add chromatic patterns based on your chosen chords and passing tones.

This process will aid you in overcoming the creative block that everyone experiences. The key to mastering it is to repeat it over and over, create many bass lines, until it becomes second nature.

▶ Example 15.8: The Creative Process

See below t the five stages of the creative process.

Stage 1: Create the Rhythm

Use freely any combination of rhtymic patterns!

Stage 2: Define the Chord

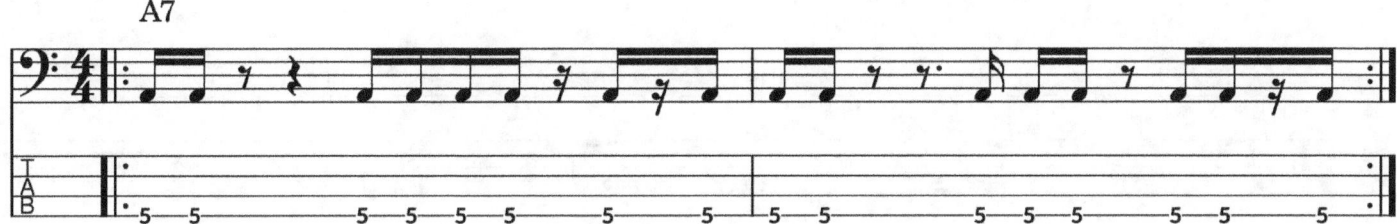

Choose a chord type and get familiar with the arpeggio and the all the scales.

Stage 3: Add the Chord Tones

Build a bass line with chord tones only.

Stage 4: Add the Passing Tones

You can add or change the previous chord tones to accomodate new ideas with passing notes.

Stage 5: Add Chromaticism

Finally add chromatic notes, between chord tones or passing notes.

Analysis of Example 15.8

Harmonic analysis

The line uses the Root and 7th of the A7 chord (A, G) plus the 6th (F♯).

The chromatic note G♯ connects the 7th (G) to the root (A), CP1: M1–B2/M2–B4.

Rhythmic analysis

RP1:   M1–B2
RP2:   M1–B1, M2–B1/B3
RP6:   M2–B2
RP9:   M2–B4
RP14: M1–B4

SUMMARY

- **We reviewed what we learned in the previous lesson and practiced longer fills. Fills can span the full measure or even be two bars long.**

- **Other chord types, aside from the 7th and the min7, require some attention to make them sound Funky. Over the Maj7 chord, it is better to avoid the major 7th, and over the min7♭5, we should use the ♭5 sparingly.**

- **The five step method can help you create a bass line until you are able to create them spontaneously.**

ETUDES

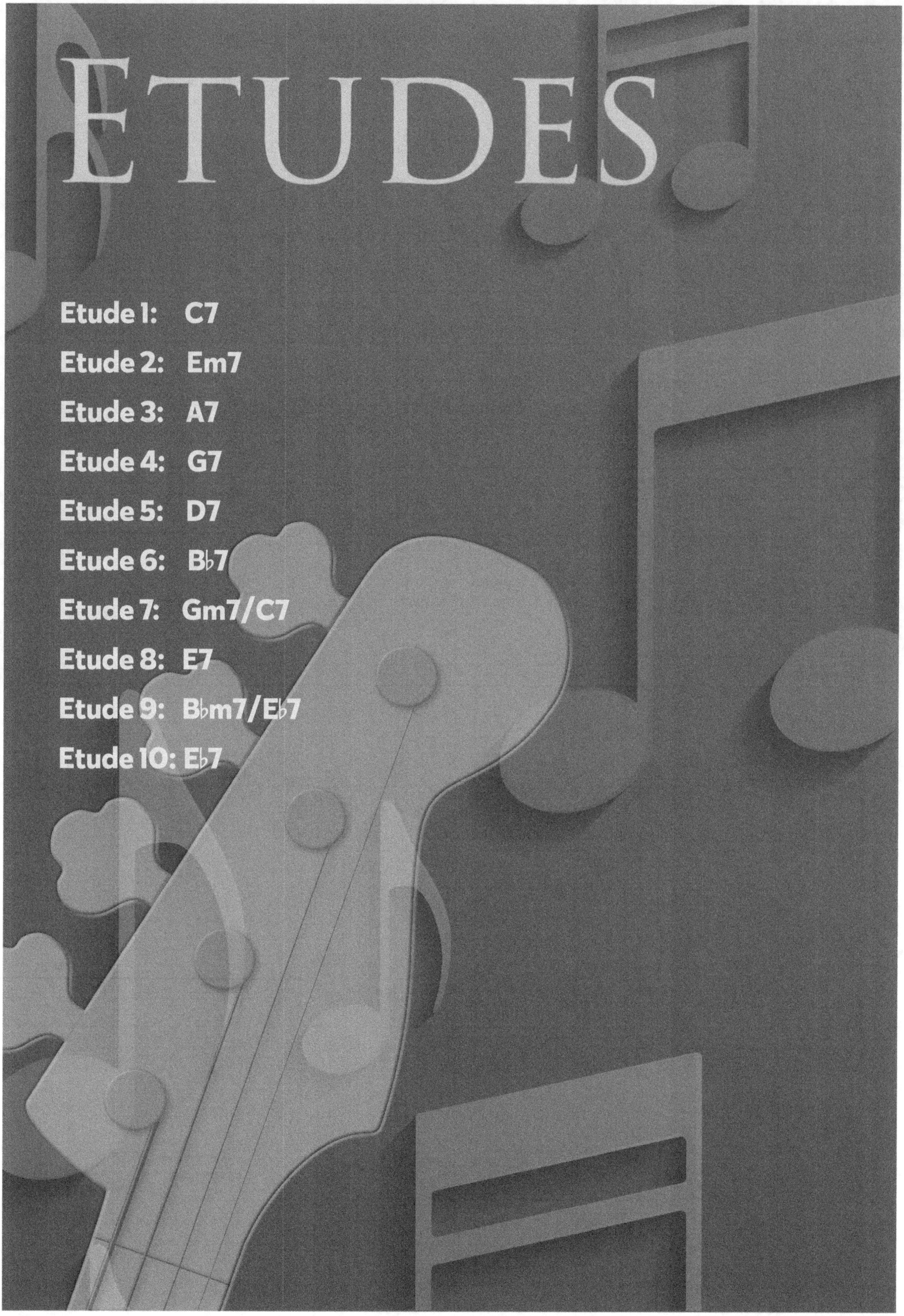

Etude 1:   C7

Etude 2:   Em7

Etude 3:   A7

Etude 4:   G7

Etude 5:   D7

Etude 6:   B♭7

Etude 7:   Gm7/C7

Etude 8:   E7

Etude 9:   B♭m7/E♭7

Etude 10: E♭7

ETUDE 1

♩ = 80

ETUDE 2

♩ = 90

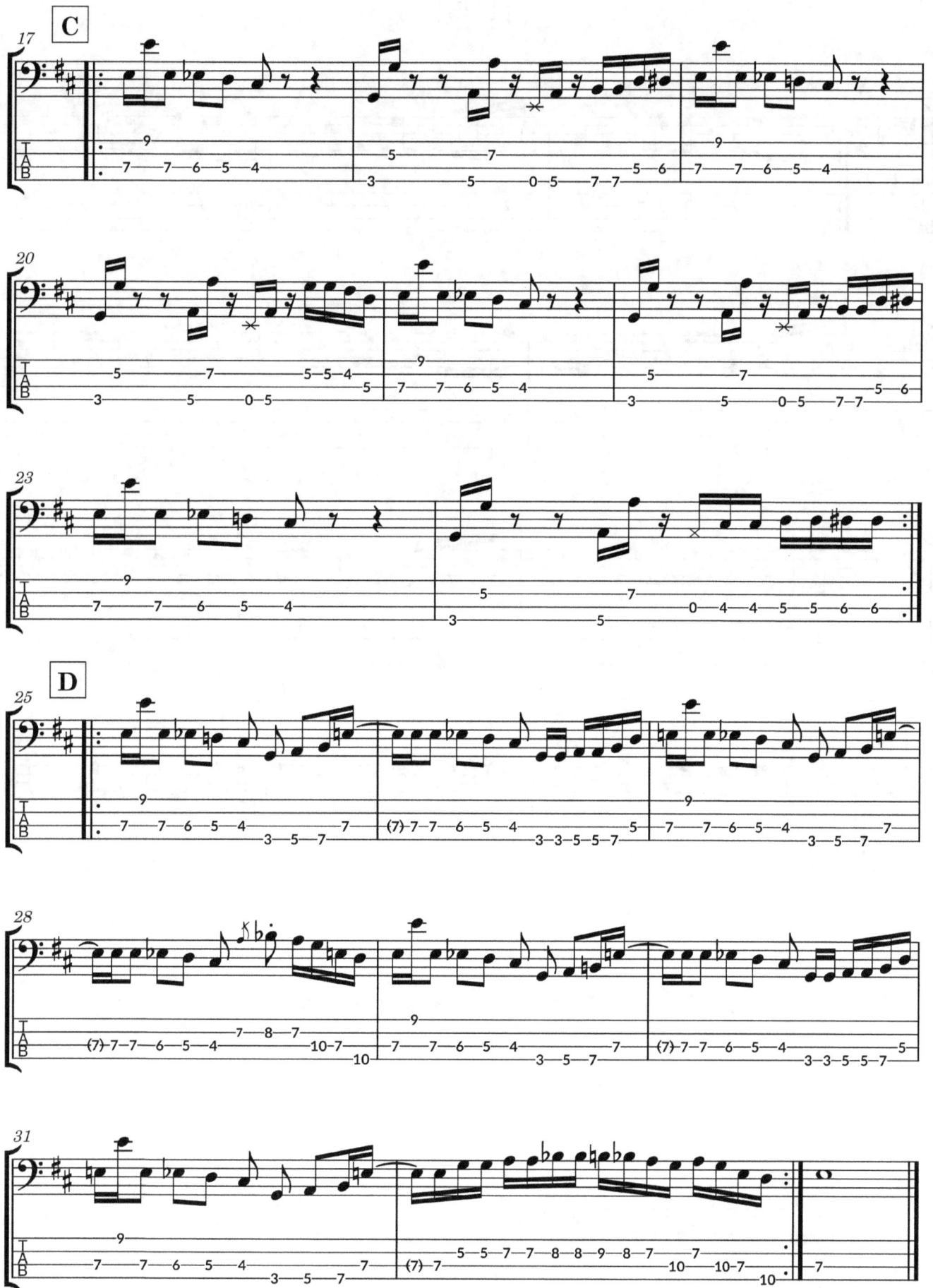

ETUDE 3

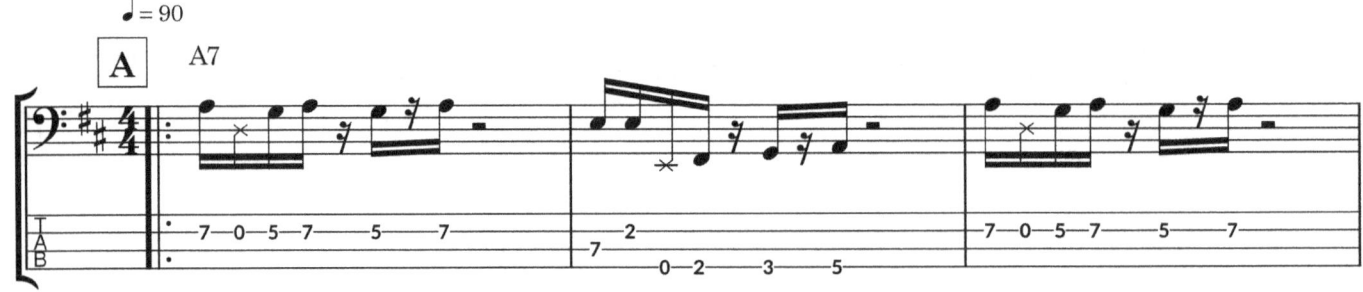

Etude 4

♩ = 90

G7

A

B

C

ETUDE 5

Etude 6

♩ = 90

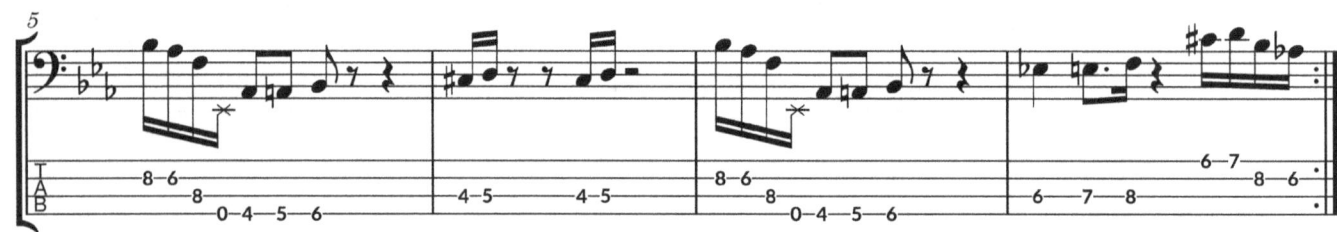

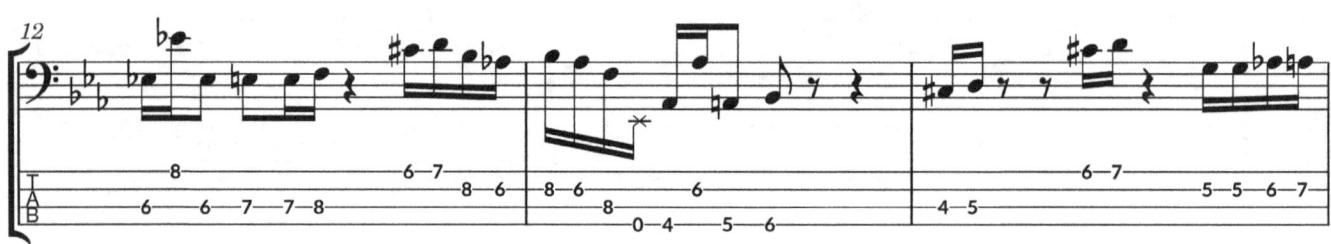

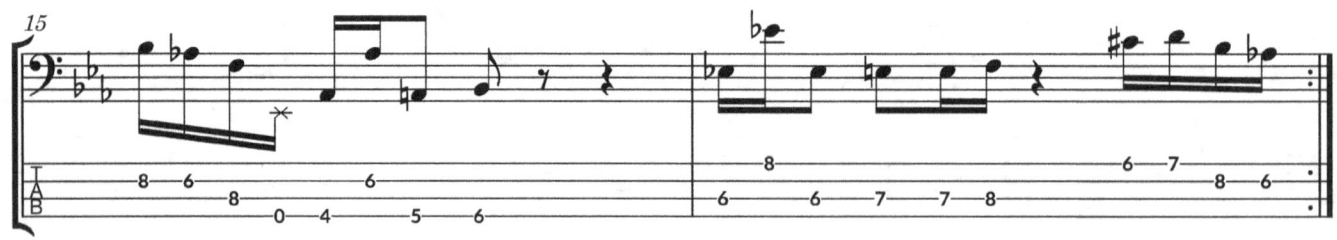

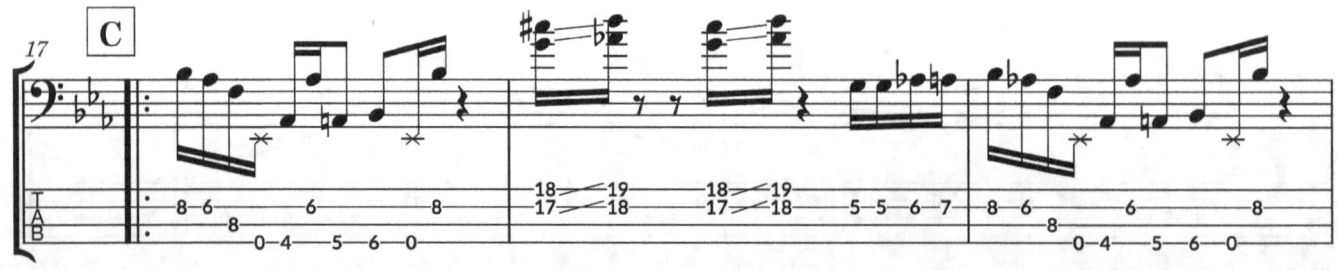

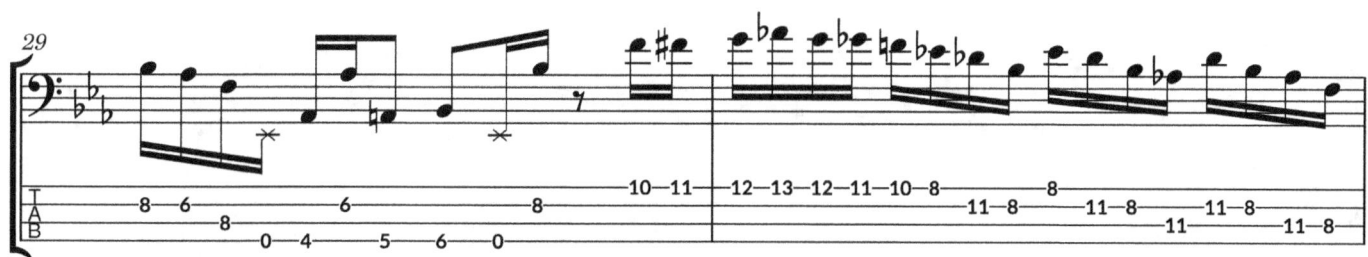

ETUDE 7

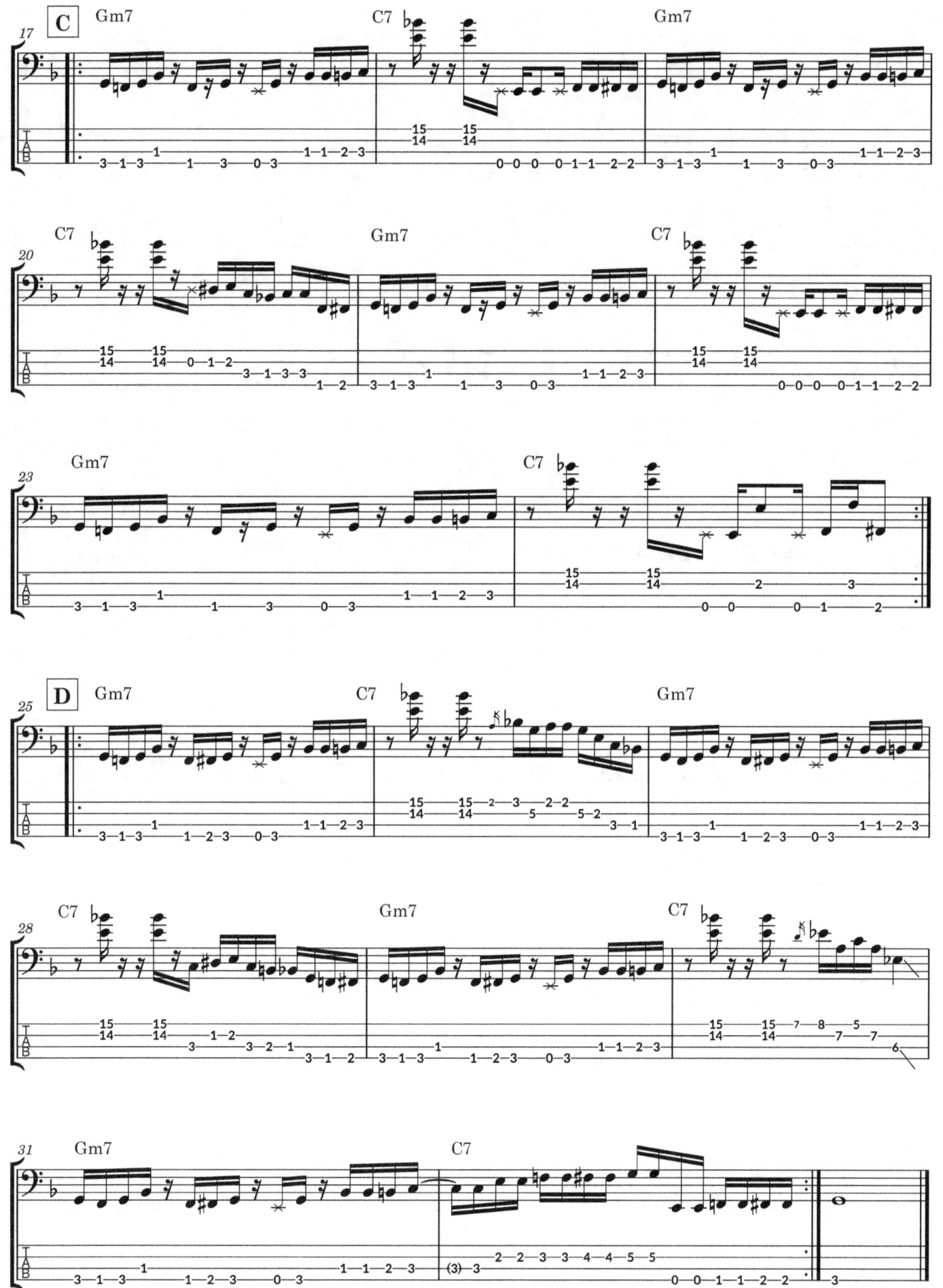

ETUDE 8

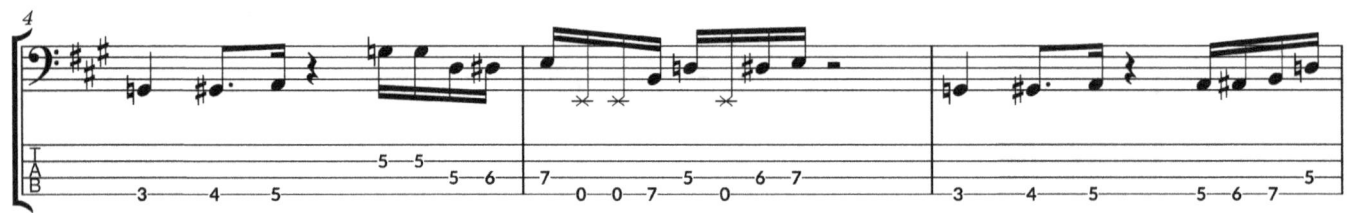

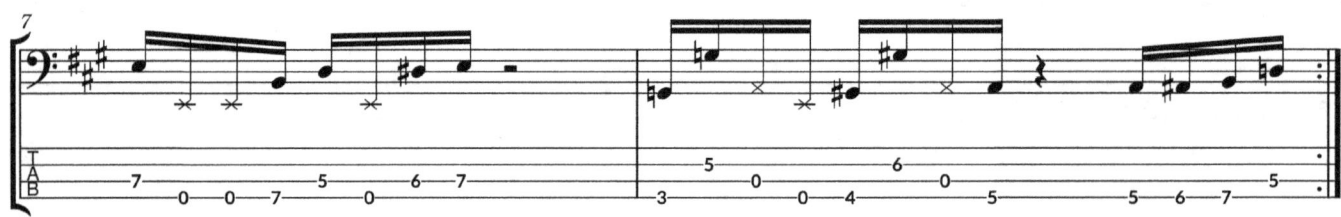

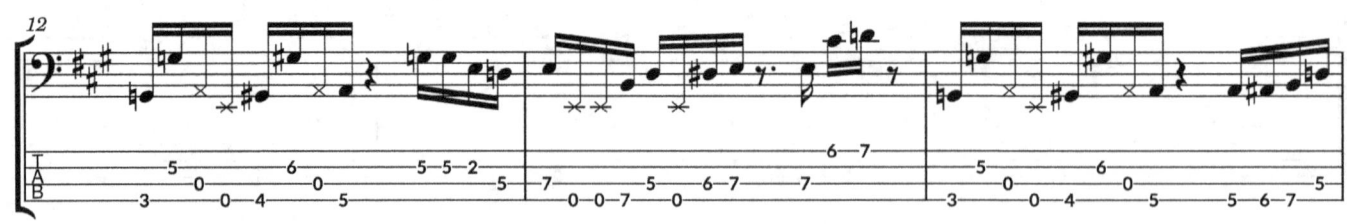

Etude 9

Etude 10

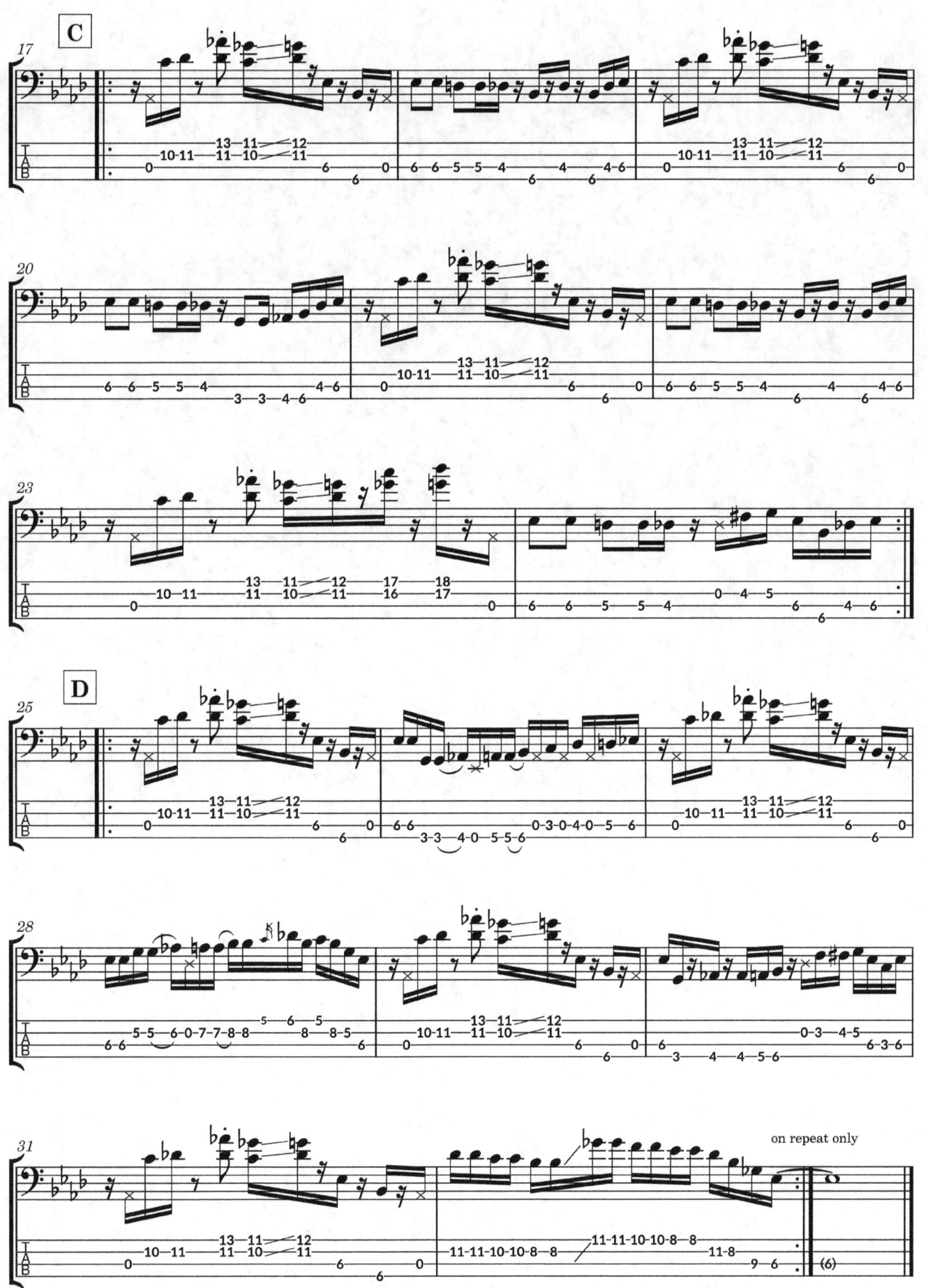

APPENDICES

LESSON 1 ADDITIONAL PRACTICE

Exercise 1.1

Exercise 1.2

Exercise 1.3

Exercise 1.4

Exercise 1.5

LESSON 2 ADDITIONAL PRACTICE

Exercise 2.1

Exercise 2.2

Exercise 2.3

Exercise 2.4

Exercise 2.5

Lesson 4 Additional Practice

Exercise 4.1

Exercise 4.2

Exercise 4.3

Exercise 4.4

Exercise 4.5

LESSON 6 ADDITIONAL PRACTICE

Exercise 6.1

Exercise 6.2

Exercise 6.3

Exercise 6.4

Exercise 6.5

LESSON 8 ADDITIONAL PRACTICE

Exercise 8.1

Exercise 8.2

Exercise 8.3

Exercise 8.4

Exercise 8.5

RHYTHMIC AND CHROMATIC PATTERNS SUMMARY

Lesson 1

RP1   RP2

Lesson 2

RP3   RP4    RP5

Lesson 3

CP1

G7

Lesson 4

RP6   RP7    RP8

RP9    RP10

Lesson 5

CP2

G7

Lesson 6

RP11   RP12    RP13

RP14

Lesson 7

CP3

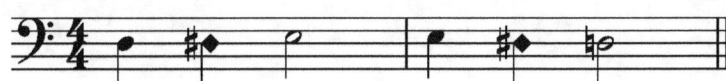

Lesson 8

Lesson 10

CP4

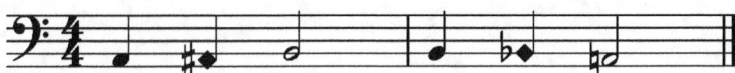

Lesson 11

CP5

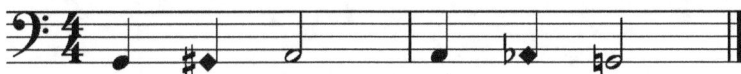

Lesson 12

CP6

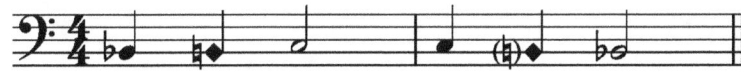